'Time and again I have seen Kate transform our talented future leaders, helping them harmonise business and personal expectations, drive their impact and relish their personal growth journey. *Get There, Love Here!* is a must read for anyone who feels frustrated or confused by the pathway to success and personal fulfilment.'

– Patricia Moore, UK Managing Director, *Turner & Townsend*

'Game-changing insights to help you bridge the gap between high achievement and happiness. Kate Trafford's wisdom and warmth shine off every page. This is a book you'll return to again and again.'

– Nadine Hack, CEO, beCause Global Consulting

'If the successful career you've been striving for feels more like a burden than a joyful opportunity, read this book and redefine success on your own terms.'

– Eleanor Ball, Founder and Director, Graphic Structures

'Insightful, powerful and brilliantly written, every word feels like Kate is talking directly to you! Brimming with inspiring guidance, and simple yet effective exercises, this book will help you discover what success really means to you – and how to get it.'

– Alaine Greaves, Finance Director, NTS

'An original and authentically brilliant route map to success that connects the dots between loving life right now and manifesting your dream destination. Ready for adventure, discovery and delight? Buckle up and enjoy the ride!'

– Mark Crossfield, coach and podcast host, Your Bravo Career

'Kate Trafford's insight and techniques for charting and navigating a successful and fulfilling career have been invaluable to me, and continue to have a positive impact years later. I am thrilled that her wisdom and expertise are now available in book form.'

– Emma Ferguson-Gould, Chief Commercial Officer, NDA

'The gentle yet powerful approach in this book is the antidote to unsustainable lifestyle "hacks" that snap you back into the grind. By the end, you'll have a new and unique road map for your most dynamic and rewarding career, and the techniques and confidence to stay on track.'

– Angela Scott, Director, Process Improvement Lab

'Packed with profound insights and practical tools, this book unveils the route map to authentic success. It will help you become the person you really want to be, have the career you really want and stay true to yourself. Learn to avoid the pitfalls and love the journey.'

– Kian Woodward, Commercial Director, Nuvia

'I've seen first-hand the impact of the ideas in this inspiring and empowering book. Kate Trafford's work with the senior leaders of Youth Fed helped us connect to our "dream destination" for the charity, move forward with even greater courage, and deliver outstanding results for the young people we serve.'

– Chris Hindley OBE, Chief Executive, Youth Fed

Get There, Love Here!

GET THERE, *Love Here!*

The busy professional's guide
to authentic, enjoyable success

KATE TRAFFORD

Get There, Love Here!

ISBN 978-1-912300-86-0
eISBN 978-1-912300-87-7

Published in 2022 by Right Book Press
Printed in the UK

A CIP record of this book is available from the British Library.

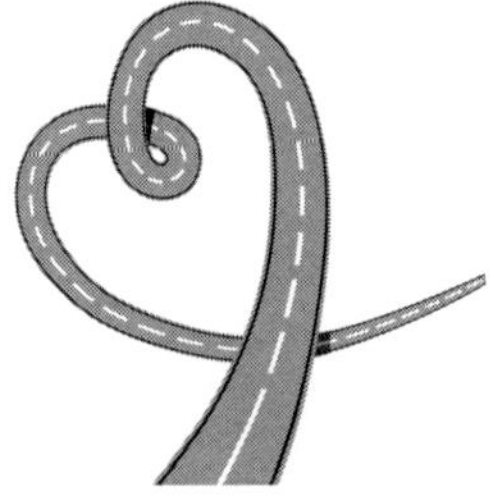

Dedicated to...

Tony, Jess and Emily
for being the heart of my convoy

John Overdurf
for helping me to find my way

Contents

PART ONE

What's Driving You?

1. ARE YOU 'ENJOYING THE JOURNEY'?

I went to the woods because I wished to live deliberately... and not, when I came to die, discover that I had not lived... I wanted to live deep and suck out all the marrow of life.

– Henry David Thoreau, Walden (1854)
American naturalist, poet and philosopher

Your journey so far

How do you know you're being successful? When you look back, a few months or perhaps a year from now, how will you know that you've been successful?

The chances are that what first comes to mind is something you'd like to have achieved. Perhaps you'll know you've been successful when you secure a promotion at work or hit the next major target in your business. Maybe you're studying right now, and success means passing with flying colours. Or perhaps you're on a mission to get a much-needed community project off the ground. Whatever you're working to achieve, you've probably got a clear idea of how you'll know when you get there.

But what happens when you expand the timeline further into the future? If you imagine looking back five years, ten years, perhaps twenty years from now, what do you hope to see? Is it still all about what you will have *achieved*, or do you also hope to look back without regret on a deeply fulfilling and joyful experience along the way? If so, then the vitally important question to consider as you pursue your current goal is this:

Are you enjoying, or merely enduring, the journey?

For over 20 years, as a coach and consultant in authentic leadership, it has been my privilege to sit in meaningful conversation with a long line of talented and capable professionals. My clients are often the emerging leaders of their organisations, high performing and high potential, talent spotted and tipped for the top. They are intelligent, capable and ambitious – both for themselves and for their organisations. They are well regarded, well rewarded and well on their way to more. By the time we first meet, when measured by their employer's and our society's standards, they'd all be described as highly successful.

If anyone might be expected to be *loving* the journey, it would be these high-achieving superstars, right? And, for some of my clients over the years, that has certainly been the case. These joyful, high-contributing, inspired leaders have taught me so much about how to achieve great things and have a great time along the way. So much so, that I sometimes wonder who should have paid who.

If that has also largely been your experience of your career so far, then this book is your chance to reflect on what has brought such joy to your journey. It's a prompt to catch yourself being brilliant – making a difference and learning and growing along the way. It will help you understand who you really are when you're at your best, so you can show up as your best self even more of the time. It will reveal your unique approach to getting the results that matter most to you, so you can replicate those results even more enjoyably and consistently. It will offer you a framework of power questions to clarify your particular 'zone of genius', so you can build a reputation for your existing sweet spot at work and support yourself in turning even more of your natural talents into fully developed strengths. You'll have the opportunity, if you wish, to reset your ambitions for your career and your life as a whole. This dream destination may be the bigger, bolder, more beautiful version of the life you are already living, or it may involve an adjustment to your direction of travel – enabling you to work towards a new dream that inspires and invigorates you. And you'll find a host of tips, insights and strategies that will help you continue to make extraordinary progress in a way that is both enjoyable and rewarding in the short run and healthy and sustainable for the long haul.

Driving hard for success

But what if this is not (yet) true for you? What if – like so many of the talented and hard-working individuals I've had the privilege of working with – the opposite is true.

Over time, I have found there is a pattern to many of my early coaching conversations. Usually, a session or two into our work together – a sense of safety established and confidentiality assured – there emerges a startlingly consistent story of frustration, overwhelm and exhaustion. Many of these intelligent, talented professionals are driving hard to get results at the expense of their health, relationships and any real sense of personal satisfaction. Sometimes with awareness, but more often unwittingly, they are sacrificing the joy available here and now in pursuit of success and happiness at some indeterminate point in the future. 'This is what it takes,' they tell me. No pain, no gain.

And so I ask,

'What does 'success' mean to you?'

Most of my clients have a ready answer. They're in a relentless race towards a clear destination – a promised promotion, a certain amount of money in the bank, a major project they can land to add another line to their already stellar CV. This next major achievement represents the point at which they will feel they've 'arrived', the point at which they'll be able to ease off a little and finally start *enjoying* their work and the life they've created for themselves. They are convinced that this next major achievement will secure their happiness. They are convinced of this *despite ample experience to the contrary.*

When I invite them to slow down long enough to reflect on their career, they see that each major achievement so far has brought at best only fleeting satisfaction. In place of the anticipated thrill of success – the longed-for and lasting sense of meaning and purpose – they acknowledge they have often experienced only temporary relief from the chronic stress. They are glad to have got something over the line, relieved that they didn't fail. Yes, there were moments of real fun and friendship along the way, and occasionally the deeper satisfaction of creativity, collaboration and contribution. But in place of the *sustained* happiness and peace of mind they believed their achievements would bring, many are left with a consistent gnawing feeling that the price they are paying for their success is way too high. This is often accompanied by a nagging background fear that everything they've achieved and accumulated so far could disappear in a heartbeat if they didn't drive so hard. What's even more sobering about this pattern is that I've had the same conversation with incredible individuals at every stage of their career, from young professionals a few years in, to senior leaders with just a few years of their career remaining.

When I ask what they want from our work together, consistent themes often emerge. They want to hear the latest persuasion techniques and productivity 'hacks' that will allow them to regain a sense of control. They are desperate to get more done in less time so that they can strike a better work/life balance, get past their current all-work-no-play grind, and carve out some quality time for themselves and their loved ones. They are hungry for leading-edge insights that might allow them to continue to outpace the competition, which they usually see not as other businesses, but as their own colleagues with whom they also need to connect and collaborate. And they want to achieve all this despite feeling exhausted and overwhelmed, and to do so while avoiding burnout. In other words, they know they are driving hard, and they want me to tell them how to drive even *harder*.

The pursuit of pleasure

At other times, a slightly different pattern emerges. These individuals similarly confess that their work is less satisfying than they'd expected it to be but have resisted the all-work-no-play approach. Instead, they choose to offset their dissatisfaction with a work-hard-play-hard approach. They are delivering in their role, and are often highly valued for their contribution, but at some level feel they are capable of so much more. They are ridiculously busy, but also bored – understimulated, despite the fast pace and endless demands.

Some of these clients choose healthy alternatives as

they look for enjoyment and fulfilment. They ratchet back their career ambitions, pouring the best of themselves into hobbies and pursuits outside work, and writing off 40-plus hours of their life each week as simply a 'necessary sacrifice'. They learn to tolerate and mask their dissatisfaction at work, to 'play the game' so they are still in the running for promotion, bonuses and other financial rewards.

Others compensate for a demanding but unfulfilling work role through barely restrained consumption – eating, drinking, partying, spending – using quick-fix pleasures to offset the pain. The pursuit of pleasure is such a popular strategy for coping with a hard-driving work role, particularly in the corporate sector, that it is often baked into the culture of the organisation. For decades rituals such as wining and dining clients and drinks after work have normalised this approach. But over time such short-term pleasures fail to compensate those spending most of their waking hours being somewhere they don't want to be, doing work they don't want to do.

The mirage of happiness

For many brilliant, hard-working professionals, there is a profoundly limiting belief at the heart of both the all-work-no-play and work-hard-play-hard strategies, one that I've heard voiced countless times. 'It's only going to be this way for a while. Once I'm more established... another promotion, maybe two... things will be different.' In other words, happiness is a destination, and it lies just beyond the next major achievement, a few weeks, a few months or a few years from now.

The reality is often very different. What starts as a temporary compromise more often than not becomes a permanent coping strategy.

Happiness becomes a shimmering mirage on the horizon of an endlessly arid emotional desert – visible, tantalising, but always *just out of reach.*

Now if you're thinking, 'Well, thanks for the pep talk, Kate. Now I'm *really* depressed!', please stay with me. I've written this book precisely because there is another way – a kinder, healthier, more enjoyable way. A way that will not only allow you to thrive and flourish but support you in achieving even more of what matters most to you. I have learned so much from clients who have navigated the opportunities and challenges of a fast-paced professional career without being ensnared by these traps. I've learned even more from my own direct experience of recognising and releasing these flawed strategies, and discovering what makes for a genuinely joyful and sustainable journey.

So, if any of the above resonates as also true for you, please read on. In the pages to come you'll find everything you need to realign and reset your journey, and shift happiness from being a mirage on the horizon to your here-and-now lived experience. What's more, the approaches we'll explore involve zero compromise on your level of contribution.

You do not have to choose between a high-achieving life and a happy one.

In fact, as research in the fields of neuroscience and positive psychology now consistently bears out, learning to enjoy the journey is your potential fast track to exceptional performance.

So slow down and settle into that feeling of resonance. Allow this to be a moment of truth, one where you're completely honest with yourself. Acknowledge that what you've been doing has not been working for you as well as you'd hoped. This is the first step in waking up to what matters most to you.

Waking up to what you really want

If you're wondering when the happy life you've been working so hard to secure will actually materialise – or even if you're in deep struggle and on the road to burnout – I want you to know that I understand. I've been where you are now and experienced my own moment of radical self-honesty. Allow me to share the turning point that enabled me to see that I was caught in a cycle of success through sacrifice, and to reset my career – and my life as a whole – onto a far more authentic, enjoyable and sustainable track.

Throughout my education, and for the first decade of my career, I gave the achievement-focused route map to success my very best shot. I worked hard, got good grades and was excited to secure a professional role with a prestigious company. And when I found that I couldn't do everything that needed to be done within the official working day, I did what school and university had trained me to do: I threw my personal time into the mix and worked *longer*.

When the promotion I earned brought with it even more to achieve, I figured out how to work *smarter*. I learned everything I could about time management and goal setting, impact and influence, and achieved even more.

This earned me another promotion, which brought with it even more to achieve. So then I worked on myself. I focused on my resilience, prioritised self-care and tried –

and failed – to achieve work/life balance. And as I went off on maternity leave at the age of 29, exhausted and with little space in my life for *anything but work*, I knew one thing for sure. Something had to change.

When I finally slowed down for long enough to think, I asked myself,

'What would success look like if you were succeeding on your own terms?'

I began to allow this experience to be a wake-up call in the most literal sense: I wanted to wake up in the morning and, in those first few moments as I pulled up my mental schedule and orientated to the day ahead, I wanted to experience *delight* – whether I woke up to a day at home nurturing my beautiful baby or to a day of challenging and rewarding professional work. I realised I was no longer willing to sacrifice today in pursuit of happiness at some imagined point in the future. Instead, I wanted to experience a sense of both achievement *and* deep satisfaction simultaneously and in an integrated way, not switching between the two in pursuit of some kind of 'balance'.

I realised that authentic success meant 'getting there' and 'loving here'.

And that's when the real work began, because I had no idea what 'there' looked like. I had no real sense of what my most authentic work might be, only that I felt called towards something. I had even less of an idea of how to achieve great things in an uncompromisingly joyful way.

With the help of a coach, I took stock of everything I knew about myself, inside and out – my personality, my strengths, my most joyful memories and everything that mattered to me in the outside world. I questioned the idea that I could meet some of my genuine needs and aspirations but not others. I explored my vision for a life of joyful contribution. And in a moment of absolute epiphany, I recognised one powerful and life-changing truth. I was not stressed and endlessly exhausted simply because I was doing too much, but because I was doing too little of what made me feel fully alive.

The more I reflected and re-evaluated my journey so far, the clearer I was able to see the truth. I'd been getting around 80 per cent of my job satisfaction from only about 20 per cent of what I'd been doing. I committed to make those elements I adored – the work that didn't really feel like work – the main focus of the next stage of my career.

The discoveries I made not only led to a radical career reset as a development consultant, they also inspired a powerful shift in my approach to parenting, releasing worry and becoming much more present to the joys of family life as they unfolded. It was the beginning of the most extraordinary – and still ongoing – journey of self-discovery and creative contribution. So profound was the impact that I often joke, 'I had my midlife crisis early!' But the truth is that what felt at first like a crisis was, in fact, an experience of authentic awakening. And I've never looked back.

And the same is possible for you. As jarring and disturbing as a significant wake-up call can be, the profoundly positive impact can be beyond measure. What may at first feel like a major problem or challenge – if navigated with curiosity and self-compassion – can become an awakening to your own untapped potential, the chance to embark on the trip of a lifetime.

You're in the perfect place to begin

If you want to set yourself on a more authentic, enjoyable and sustainable path, is it always necessary to make a radical change? *Absolutely not.* Most of my coaching clients use the discoveries they make – about themselves and what matters most – to find what they are looking for *right where they are.* Most recognise that they are already on their authentic path but meeting other people's demands at the expense of contributing their most authentic work. Others find that they are simply approaching their work in an unsustainable way, succumbing to the 'always on' culture that suggests that giving your best means giving until you can give no more. You may already be the right person in the right place. This reset is less about needing a change of scenery, and more about *seeing where you are with new eyes.*

The ideas, strategies and stories you'll find in the pages that follow will support you in creating and experiencing your most authentic career, and integrating that rewarding work into a life that you love. Whether you're already riding high with magnificent momentum, or burning yourself out just to keep up, this book will help you fully claim the journey as your own, and bring it to life with your own gifts, your own passions and your own desire to make a difference. It will help you see the debilitating paradigm that often robs life – particularly corporate life – of joy and meaning, and offer you instead a far more inspiring and empowering perspective.

Life need not be a relentless race.
Life can be an authentic adventure.

Most of all, I hope this book will help you to see your own true worth, and to be willing to explore and express your unique brilliance every day, for your own joy and to the benefit of the world around you.

Start a travel log

Before we head out on our explorations together, one quick suggestion to help you make the most of this book. Throughout you'll find a series of questions and activities, all marked out for your attention using the following icon.

Some of these exercises are active, others more reflective. Each is designed to take you deeper and closer to who you really are and what you most want to create and experience from here.

With this in mind, I recommend you keep a 'travel log' – a record of your ideas, your discoveries, your 'Aha!' moments along the way. Treat yourself to a new notebook, one that looks and feels good in your hands, and carry it with you.

Feel free to read the book through from cover to cover first, if you prefer, and then *return to these marked-out activities later*. Consider discussing these questions and your insights with a friend – someone you trust to be objective, but also to have your best interests at heart – but please do make notes. This book will offer you a framework, a new route map to authentic success, but the content will be uniquely your own.

As your insights and awareness grow, you'll reach a

tipping point where suddenly the themes and patterns that have underpinned your journey so far become clear. You'll be able to discern which aspects were really 'you' and which you were simply trained to pursue. And with that, you'll discover your unique criteria for your most authentic adventure from here. You'll recognise yourself so clearly in what you find that you may wonder how you missed it before.

So, what if you could truly love your career journey and your life as a whole? What if you could access the bliss of enjoyable and sustainable success? Not only is this entirely possible; it's what you were born for! Making this shift is what the rest of this book is all about.

Here's where we're headed

In the pages that follow, you will discover...

- ✦ A more authentic route map to success, guiding you towards your most extraordinary adventure from here.
- ✦ How to put your true self in the driving seat and recognise and cultivate your natural 'zone of genius'.
- ✦ How to envision your dream destination, and how to distinguish this authentic goal from what you may have been trained to pursue.
- ✦ How to listen to your inner satnav so you can navigate uncertainty with courage and confidence.
- ✦ How to harness the power of your built-in autopilot so you can experience effortless success, or at least set yourself up to 'effort' less.
- ✦ How to overcome inertia, soup up your systems and make progress like a pro.
- ✦ How to set yourself up for long-haul success so you can enjoy the drive of your life.

Let the journey begin!

2. Driving (Too) Hard for Success

It's good to have an end to journey towards; but it is the journey that matters, in the end.

– Ursula Le Guin, *The Left Hand of Darkness* (1969)
American novelist and poet

No licence? No problem

Do you know how to drive? For the purposes of this book, I'm going to assume the answer is 'yes' and ask you to gloss over my assumption if the answer is 'no'. After all, even if you are not a licence holder yourself, you've almost certainly seen it done often enough to have a grasp of the basics. You've been on enough road trips and watched enough movies to know how to travel well.

You already know the power of a clear and compelling destination. Yes, it can be blissful to take the scenic route, with no purpose beyond being fully present to the wonders of this extraordinary world we live in. But to experience yourself as the creator of your own journey – to feel like you are truly in the driving seat, experiencing the rich rewards of discovery, growth and contribution – it helps to know where you're headed. Arriving at an unexpectedly delightful destination by chance can be an absolute thrill, but the thrill can be even greater when you arrive at a destination that was once just a dream.

As an experienced traveller you also know that, even when your destination is not yet clear, you can make excellent progress *and* have a fabulous time along the way. At first, a general direction of travel is enough: I could set out from my home in the north-west of England and head further north for quite some time before needing to be any more specific than 'I'd like to see Scotland'. But as you make progress, crossroads appear that must be navigated. You need some way of knowing which way to turn. So, you make finer distinctions along the way, clarifying where you *really* want to go and what you truly wish to experience.

Discerning your authentic preferences allows you to make intelligent and heartfelt choices as your journey unfolds.

You know that every destination you reach is also a departure point. You understand that, each time you complete a leg of your journey, your horizon shifts. You have a new vantage point on what you'd most like to achieve and experience in the next stage. Chatting with the 'locals', you pick up on insights as to the best way forward: shortcuts, more detailed maps, local knowledge you could not have anticipated or even known you might need. You may even find that, as you scan the far horizon, you suddenly see a new and even more compelling destination than the one you originally envisioned. This new dream destination may be beyond anything you could previously imagine, but now there it is, clearly visible and calling your name.

Your on-the-road experience so far also tells you that the journey is not only a linear progression from A to B. It also cycles between active phases of forward motion and inactive phases that allow you to rest, reflect and refocus. At times, you churn up the miles, foot to the floor and thrilled by the ride. At other times you slow down, the better to take everything in or to navigate tricky terrain. Eventually, you pull over for a rest stop. You take care of your vehicle and yourself. Only when you're refuelled, refreshed and raring to go do you set out once again, confident you'll swiftly regain your momentum. On a road trip, you understand that honouring this natural cycle – shifting continuously between rest/reflection and forward motion – is essential to your journey. Not only do both aspects make your progress sustainable, but they also make it more enjoyable, and they ensure you stay on track with what matters most to you. When you're in it for the long haul, the fundamentals of travelling well are self-evident.

You can't simply go fast if you want to go far.

The true gift of the journey

Cast your mind back to the most wonderful road trip you've ever taken. You'll see clearly that the purpose of your journey is often far deeper and more meaningful than simply wanting to be somewhere other than where you are. In fact, quite often your road trip will be circular: you'll explore and enjoy a whole series of destinations, and then deliberately and joyfully arrive right back where you started.

The true gift of the journey is not only that you reach your destination, but that you are transformed by your travels.

The memories you make, the people you meet and the experiences you have all change you. The 'you' that comes home from a magnificent road trip is not the same 'you' that set out. As you embrace the adventures of an open road, you not only see new sights – you see your world with new eyes.

You know what makes for a miserable journey too. A car full of back seat drivers, all arguing about which route you should take. Squabbling kids asking, 'Are we there yet?' when you've barely left the driveway. Listening to the creaks and clunks of your vehicle and wondering if it might let you down at any moment. Mentally sniping at other road users. Constantly comparing where you are with where you think you should be.

These, and many other truths, are obvious when considering a literal road trip. But if you've lost sight of these 'truths' when it comes to the journey of life, you're in good company.

Having had the opportunity of working with hundreds of established and emerging leaders at this point, I can say one thing for sure: *if we don't wake ourselves up, life has a way of doing it for us.*

If you've lost your way, you're in good company

By the time we begin our work, my clients – particularly those more established in their career – are often navigating what is simply the latest in a whole series of potential wake-up calls, previously batted away to allow a swift return to business as usual. Yes, there are those who are genuinely and deeply satisfied in both their professional and personal lives, inspired by a sense of so much they still want to accomplish and relishing the prospect of a rich and rewarding retirement. But at times, and more often than I'd ever imagined, a different story emerges – one of broken relationships, failing health and existential angst – all hidden behind a mask of high-achieving invincibility.

This challenging emotional terrain is often further complicated by feelings of anger, sadness and guilt. As one executive client confided, 'I understand the privilege of my position. I do know how lucky I am. It's just that... well... I've worked so hard my entire life to get here, done everything I was supposed to do, made huge sacrifices along the way... I guess I thought at some point all this would pay off and I'd be happy. But the truth is, *I'm still waiting.*'

He was shocked when I assured him that he was far from alone in this, when I explained that sadly his experience is one shared with me many times before. 'So, why are we not talking about this?' he asked. 'Maybe if we could be honest with one another, acknowledge that we're racing around thinking "There's got to be more to life than this", we'd find new ways of doing things. Then, soon, there *would* be more to life than this.'

There are real reasons why so few of us are 'talking about this', why we ignore and override our intuition when it tells us that a better way must be possible – a kinder, more humane and even more productive way. And it all begins with the training you received as a learner driver.

The rules of the road

From almost the moment you were born, those around you sought to guide your choices. If you were fortunate, this guidance will have come from well-meaning adults with your best interests at heart: parents or caregivers, teachers, spiritual guides, youth leaders and other authority figures wanting to give you the best start in life and offer you the clearest possible route map to ultimate success and happiness. But even in this best-case scenario, the guidance you received will also have reflected the values and expectations of your family, your community and society at large. The resulting 'rules of the road' vary from culture to culture, and at times by other factors, such as different rules for girls and boys. But, for many of the busy professionals I work with in the UK, the early driver training went something like this:

- **Rule 1:** Pay attention to the people around you. We've been here longer than you have. We know more about how life really works than you do. Your own wants, instincts and impulses may feel powerful but they cannot be trusted. Your feelings will lead you astray from what you need to learn to get along with others and fit in to the structures that have been put in place for you.
- **Rule 2:** Do as you are told. Meet our expectations and you'll be rewarded. Ignore them and there will be consequences.
- **Rule 3:** Work hard. Get a good education. Yes, we want you to have friends, but the rest of your life depends upon what you achieve in school. You must be willing to sacrifice fun and friendship in favour of getting results. If you're one of the rare few with an obvious and exceptional talent for sport or the creative arts, we'll let you know. But otherwise stick with the academic subjects. These are useful and will enable you to be useful when you leave school.
- **Rule 4:** Choose a well-paved, well-signposted route to success. Work hard enough for long enough and you may have the chance of a place at university. Keep working hard, keep excelling, and you'll secure a professional career. Yes, the competition is intense, but

it's not forever. Just keep going and you can be one of the winners!

- **Rule 5:** Don't worry about the losers. They are not your concern. There is only so much success to go around, so keep your eyes on the prize and claim your share.
- **Rule 6:** Let people know you're winning by buying your own home, wearing the right clothes, eating at the right restaurants, driving the right car. We'll helpfully show you, in every ad break, which is the right home, the right clothes, the right restaurant, the right car.
- **Rule 7:** Don't make it look easy, otherwise people will question your commitment and contribution.
- **Rule 8:** Make it look easy, otherwise people will question your competence and resilience.
- **Rule 9:** Family matters. Along the way, be sure to meet the right person, have 2.4 children and take care of your parents. Don't let your work get in the way of family, but don't let family get in the way of your work.
- **Rule 10:** Keep your foot to the floor. You can have it all. You just have to earn it, and keep earning it, every single day. Life may be a journey, but it's a particular *kind* of journey: life is a *race*.

Now maybe some of these 'rules' feel familiar to you, and others thankfully don't. But if even a few of them resonate as true for you, we've got work to do. These ways of relating to yourself, your work and the world are rooted in what author Gill Edwards (2009) calls 'taming, blaming and shaming'. They may be well intentioned, designed to keep you safe, shared to support your success. But they train you to look outside of yourself for answers – guiding you away from your own instincts and intuition, your own loving impulses, the potential for a life filled with meaning, joy and authentic contribution.

I'm not criticising anyone's caregivers, or even railing against society in general. It's certainly possible to get a lot done with the above rules in place, at least for a good few years. And besides, most of us parent, teach and manage as we were conditioned to, in accordance with the beliefs and values of our family of origin, the education system and even our particular industry or work sector. Few people deeply and consciously question the world view that drives their decisions (though the fact that you are reading this book marks *you* out as one of the few that do). And that's why recognising the limitations of these well-intentioned rules is also an extraordinary opportunity.

The more people who wake up to the limits of their conditioned world view, and choose to *redefine success on their own terms*, the more people there will be in the world showing others that a different way – a more authentic, joyful, sustainable way – is possible.

Life as a busy professional has the potential to be an extraordinarily rich and rewarding experience. I want to shout from the rooftops about the magic that happens when an individual's purpose, values and talents align with those of their team or organisation. My point is simply this. Joyful contribution may be your birthright but, if even a few of the rules of the road above resonated with you, then it's crucial to recognise one thing. You were not trained to love the journey. You were trained for *driving hard*.

You know you're driving hard when...

How do you know when you're driving hard? Here are a few of the most common signs:

- You feel stressed as you clock-watch your way to a looming deadline.
- You feel tired, perhaps even exhausted, and would love to take a break but it seems like there's no time to slow down.
- You take on more and more – to keep your boss or clients happy, to impress others by 'going above and beyond' or simply because you don't feel you can say no – and then feel burdened, obligated and resentful.
- You get bogged down in the day-to-day challenges, fire-fighting problem after problem, knowing at some level that you've lost perspective. You wish you had the headspace to think more strategically – to plan, reflect and connect – but there's rarely the time for that.
- You criticise yourself for not getting more done, or others for not doing their fair share.
- You consider asking for help, or renegotiating timescales and deliverables, but hesitate. You're concerned that others may think you're not coping or not pulling your weight. Instead, you keep on driving harder and harder, hoping that somehow, you'll find a way through.
- You work excessive hours, then collapse in the evenings into a fitful attempt to recover. You binge-watch television or scroll on social media, drawing little satisfaction from either.
- You keep yourself going during the week with thoughts of the weekend, when you hope to have fun and recharge your batteries, but often find yourself recreating the same pattern at home as you experience

at work. You try to catch up on everything that needs to be done. Even spending time with your friends and loved ones sometimes feels like an item on your overly long to-do list. There is never enough time for it all.

- Your fatigue becomes chronic until, at last, you can take a holiday. When you do, your mind continually wanders to what might be going on at work without you. You may or may not resist the urge to check your phone and emails, and even if you do resist it takes most of the first week just to unwind. In the best-case scenario, you accomplish the blissful state of deep relaxation you hoped for, returning refreshed and revitalised. But you are back at your desk for a few days, perhaps even a few hours, before your holiday starts to feel like a distant memory.
- Deep down, you know you're not happy, but you also know you have so much to be grateful for, and so much more than many others. And that means your unhappiness cannot be spoken of or even fully acknowledged. To do so triggers feelings of guilt and shame. You have a word with yourself and drive on in silence.
- You recognise that your way of working and living is not sustainable for the long haul, and you sometimes worry about burnout or the long-term impact on your health and relationships. But so much is expected of you, and you expect so much of yourself, that you soothe yourself from these fearful thoughts with pleasurable distractions – eating, drinking, gossiping, spending. You worry because you know that these 'pleasures' create problems of their own. You feel sure there must be more to life.

So why is it that, despite your best efforts and your dedication in following the rules of the road, you're not yet enjoying the sustainable and deeply satisfying success you deserve? Why, despite driving so hard, are you still not *happy*?

The map is the trap

With so much taming, blaming and shaming built into the rules you were given, it would be easy to jump to faulty conclusions, as many do. You could assume that any unhappiness you're experiencing is because of some personal flaw or failing, particularly if the back seat drivers in your head are saying, 'You just need to step up, dig deep, double down. You should be grateful, keep the faith, wait your turn!' But this is absolutely *not* the case.

**It is not you that is flawed,
but the fundamental route map
to success you were given.**

No matter how hard you try, a route map that demands continuous, significant and ongoing sacrifice will never get you where you want to be, if where you want to be includes a happy, healthy, thriving you. Here's why.

The fundamental promise of driving hard is that ultimately it will lead you to happiness. The harder you drive, the more you will achieve. And the more you achieve, the happier you will be.

At first glance this seems reasonable. Achievement *does feel good*. And we all know it can feel very good, at least temporarily, to achieve a significant goal. What's more, our society does visibly reward 'high achievers'. High-achieving students often secure places at the best schools. High-achieving graduates land the best professional opportunities. High-achieving employees get promoted. High-achieving managers are chosen by shareholders and partners to be high-achieving leaders. Achievement brings opportunity.

At the early stages of the 'race', moving through our education system, success means simply the opportunity to proceed to the next stage: the chance to work towards a higher level of achievement and to become even more skilled and knowledgeable along the way. But once you join the world of work, if you can keep up the pace, the rewards become more tangible. You'll likely receive a pay rise – and with it, a boost to your standard of living – at every subsequent stage.

On our society's route map to success, hard work and sacrifice lead to achievement, which leads to recognition and reward, which lead to a high standard of living. And this, at least in theory, leads to happiness. But can you see the fundamental flaws with this strategy?

First, little if anything is said to acknowledge that only a small proportion of these hard-driving professionals progress at every stage, and even less is said about the prospects for those who don't. Maybe you're OK with that, providing you're one of the 'winners'. But even for those who do move forward in this achievement-driven model, the promised prize of *sustained happiness* rarely materialises. At every new stage the demand increases, and with it the expected level of commitment, impact and sacrifice. Gradually, it becomes abundantly clear that, beyond the point at which your basic needs are met...

A higher *standard of living* does not necessarily translate into a higher *quality of life*.

Your quality of life is fundamentally the quality of your *emotional* experience along the way. It is underpinned by how you feel, moment by moment, day by day. If you sacrifice the joy available to you here and now in pursuit of happiness at some imagined point in the future, you potentially commit yourself to a lifelong experience of emotional drought, eased only by quick-fix pleasures and the rare and fleeting thrill of a significant 'win'.

The pursuit of happiness

Am I questioning the pursuit of happiness, regarded as such a fundamental human right as to be enshrined in the poetic words of the US Constitution? Yes, I am, if the pursuit is not driven by joy along the way.

As we've already seen, the pursuit of happiness can easily translate into a lifelong reaching for a mirage on the horizon, with happiness positioned at or just beyond the next major achievement. In the conditioned route map to success your here-and-now connection to joy is replaced by an unconscious commitment to drive hard for results. You're trained to sacrifice today in pursuit of a better tomorrow.

If we gave the pursuit of happiness a voice, it might sound something like this:

- I'll be happy when I'm done with my studies.
- I'll be happy when I land a great job.
- I'll be happy when I get promoted.
- I'll be happy when the house purchase goes through.
- I'll be happy when I have 'amount X' in the bank.
- I'll be happy when I meet the love of my life.
- I'll be happy when I have a family of my own.
- I'll be happy when we're through this tricky parenting phase.

- I'll be happy when I secure my first real leadership role.
- I'll be happy when I make it onto the board.
- I'll be happy when I retire.

Always hard driving, and only fleetingly 'arriving', each moment of celebration giving way to the next belief about what needs to be true before we can really love the journey.

We've already acknowledged that achievement alone is no guarantee of happiness. No matter how sizeable the win, or how significant the milestone, there will always be more to achieve. But driving hard towards milestones becomes a habit, and the stories we tell ourselves – the endless stream of automatic thoughts that run through our minds all day every day – keep the momentum going.

'I'll be happy when _______________' statements sound hopeful. So, too, do the many variations on the same theme:

- 'I'll be confident when _______________.'
- 'I'll be secure when _______________.'
- 'I'll feel good about myself when _______________.'

But each of these declarations is a negative affirmation. Every time you tell yourself, 'I'll be happy/confident/secure or feel good about myself when _______________', you are affirming that you *can't* feel happy/confident/secure/good about yourself *now*. You are unknowingly – but quite literally – hypnotising yourself into an ongoing experience of sadness, stress and self-doubt.

Breaking this chain of pain involves pausing to question your 'no pain, no gain' programming.

It requires you to sanity-check the belief that to get what you want in one area of your life you must compromise on another. It asks you to challenge the idea that success always demands sacrifice. And the easiest way to do this is to ask yourself one simple question: 'Does that truly reflect my own experience?'

If you are anything like me (and every client I have ever asked) you will have experienced days where you achieved something extraordinary but doing so cost you very little. Yes, you poured an enormous amount of energy into making the magic happen, but the energy arose spontaneously in the moment it was needed. You felt uplifted and inspired – no hint of the need to 'dig deep' or drive hard. Just the thrill of engaging with an outcome that was authentically meaningful to you.

Perhaps at the end of that long day you were tired but still buzzing. You were ready to take yourself off to bed, but with no sign of the kind of bone-tired exhaustion you might previously have experienced following far lower levels of exertion. Perhaps you wound down for the evening by sharing your experience with a friend or loved one, reliving the joy of it all over again, before settling down to a good night's sleep. And maybe you noticed the next day that, despite expending all that energy, you were invigorated, energised and ready for more.

You already know – from your own direct experience – that it is entirely possible to achieve great things while enjoying laughter, enthusiasm and camaraderie along the way. And that means you already know that *happiness need not be pursued.*

Happiness is not a destination,
but a here-and-now way of travel.

Getting there and loving here

You were conditioned to believe that high achievement – driving hard for results at almost any cost – would eventually lead to happiness. But if, like many others, you've found that the happiness you were promised has become that mirage on the horizon – a tantalising vision that moves further away no matter how hard you try – then it's time to question that well-intentioned but misguided conditioning.

The exciting truth is that we can turn this equation around:

High achievement may not guarantee your happiness, but here-and-now happiness can drive extraordinary achievement.

Self-care, fun and authentic self-expression are not distractions from high performance but the key drivers of your sustainable and stellar success.

You deserve to get the results that matter most to you and be happy along the way. You deserve a journey rich with the joy of authentic accomplishment, rooted in ease and excitement. You deserve to get there *and* love here.

3. From Willpower to Thrill Power

Don't ask yourself what the world needs. Ask yourself what makes you come alive, and go do that, because what the world needs is people who have come alive.

– attributed to author, philosopher and civil rights leader Howard Thurman by Gil Bailie in *Violence Unveiled* (1995)

Are you attempting a getaway?

Imagine for a moment that you're standing on a busy city street. You hail a cab. The driver pulls over and asks, 'Where to?' and you reply, 'Not here.'

How do you think the driver would respond? They might give you a puzzled or frustrated look. They might point out that 'Not here' is not a destination, and ask you again. Or perhaps they'd recognise that 'Not here' is a fine answer in a crisis, assume you're in trouble and just get moving. You could clock up a lot of miles and pay a huge price without needing to be any more specific than 'Not here'. You wouldn't have achieved or enjoyed much on such a directionless journey, but you'd be moving. And sometimes, perhaps especially in the world of work, we can convince ourselves that moving at speed is the same as making progress. Making a 'getaway' from where you are now is fine in a crisis but lurching from crisis to crisis is no way to live your life.

Getting away *from* where you are and moving towards your preferred destination are two very different experiences. Even if the result is the same, even if the actions you take are the same, the *direction* of your motivation – away from what you don't want or towards what you do want – fundamentally dictates the quality of your experience along the way.

For example, let's say you sign up for membership at your local gym. If this action is 'away from' motivated, you'll be trying to get away from one of two things: a here-and-now unwanted situation – feeling sick and tired, unhappy with your reflection in the mirror or the stern look on your doctor's face as they shared your latest blood test results – or an unwanted projection of where you're headed – future burnout, future obesity, a future heart attack – if you don't make a change. The chances are you'll tap into your willpower and grind out the exercise as a necessary evil, all the while comparing yourself unfavourably with the fitter, stronger, slimmer gym members and wondering why the hell they fill these places with so many mirrors.

On the other hand, if your motivation direction is 'towards', you'll be inspired by taking good care of this one precious vehicle you've been gifted for this lifetime. You'll be moving towards a future vision of the vibrantly healthy, slim and strong, good-feeling body you want to allow to emerge. You'll experiment with the different workouts and classes to find the ones you most enjoy and see your current status as simply the 'before picture' of the wonderful journey you're undertaking. You'll appreciate the mirrors for helping you practise good form, and you'll enjoy seeing the visible progress you are making. Same decision (join a gym), same action (exercise), totally different experience.

It is the direction of your motivation – away from or towards – that determines whether you enjoy the journey or merely endure it.

Driving yourself to take action by making where you are now wrong, inadequate or unacceptable in some way is *motivation through misery*. When you push against the way things are – endlessly waiting for something to be over – the ongoing experience is one dominated by anxiety, frustration and stress. You dig deep and drive hard, drawing on your willpower to do what needs to be done, attempting to silence the voice in your head that tells you it'll never be enough. You focus on escaping this uncomfortable moment, avoiding what you *don't* want. You feel compelled to act now, to avoid a myriad of negative future consequences. Your actions are motivated by desperation, driven by fear.

In contrast, when you are moving in the direction of a meaningful, new-and-improved destination – while *continuing to take delight in where you already are* – you experience both the perfect peace and the pure potential of each moment. You feel like the right person in the right place at the right time. You are present to both what is wonderful about where you are now *and* to the 'more' that is possible. You appreciate your life and everyone in it, including yourself. You focus on creating and experiencing what you do want. You feel pulled forward by your vision for the future. You are clear minded about the chance to make progress right here, right now. You see the gap between where you are and where you want to be as a delicious opportunity to realise any untapped potential, and to live fully and vibrantly along the way. Your actions are motivated by *inspiration*, driven by *love*.

So, we come to the single most important distinction you can make if you truly want to drive for your dreams and love the journey. The answer to the question 'How can I get there, and love here?' lies in considering not only your direction of travel (where you are going), but also your *direction of motivation* (how you drive yourself along the way). Are you driving hard to get away from what you dislike about where you are now and avoid any imagined future problems or are you relishing this moment, joyfully journeying towards the new destination you most wish to create and experience?

Are your decisions motivated by desperation or inspiration? Are you driven by fear or by love?

Willpower alone won't get you there

There's no doubt that a great deal can be achieved when you're driven by desperation. The burst of energy accessed each time you remind yourself of the urgent need for action can be intense, powerful, primal. And when you dig deep and grind it out, you're rewarded not only by the results you get but by the short-term boost to your self-esteem that comes from living up to years of conditioning that tells you, 'When the going gets tough, the tough get going.'

But strategies for success that are rooted in endless struggle are doomed to fail. Why? Because they leave you with no choice but to draw on your willpower over and over again, all day every day, in an increasingly stressful attempt to keep any promises you made to yourself or others. And therein lies a significant problem:

Willpower is a finite resource.

If you've ever tried to break an unwanted habit of any kind, you already know this. So, whether your valiant attempts to make a change end abruptly or through a slow and painful decline remains to be seen. But if you rely on willpower alone, your efforts will almost certainly go unrewarded in the long haul. Like the energy stored in your car battery, willpower is an incredible resource you can draw on when truly required. It can spark action and help get you moving. But when it's gone, it's gone.

Why is willpower a limited resource? The answer lies in the mental imagery that is the source of your motivation. When desperation gets you started, the imagery imprinted on your mind is of something *unwanted*. Using our gym example above, this would be your unacceptable reflection in the mirror, your doctor's stern face or the numbers on your blood test results. This image then triggers a mental 'disaster movie' of where you're likely to end up if you don't turn things around. This painful mental movie is the source of your motivation because it represents the unacceptable condition that must be changed, and it runs like a GIF file over and over again to keep you alert to the dangers of complacency and inaction.

Having your motivation depend on something you are trying to *avoid* – your current unwanted situation or an even scarier future destination – is deeply problematic. That's because:

Unless something else kicks in to energise and sustain your progress, your motivation is destined to disappear, and you're likely to find yourself right back where you started, or worse.

There are three main reasons why. The first reason is the problem of *success*. What happens if, through grit and determination, you do achieve some initial beneficial results? Seeing your struggle rewarded may give you a boost at first – after all, your hard work is paying off. But as you continue to drive hard to make progress, your success moves you further and further away from the unwanted circumstances that were the original source of your motivation. As a result, suddenly or slowly over time, your desperation eases. You're no longer quite so afraid – no longer quite so stressed by where you are, or anxious about the trajectory you're on – and therefore no longer quite so motivated. Before you know it, you're back where you started, or worse – until desperation kicks back in and the cycle begins again.

The second reason is the problem of *sustainability*. The effort involved in maintaining a strict regimen – especially one that requires rigid self-discipline – is enormous. This is because you need to find the energy both to drive the action you take and to overcome your internal resistance. It's like trying to drive with your handbrake still on. So, what happens if, despite your grit and determination, you *don't* make much progress? Such a high level of discomfort and deprivation is not sustainable for the long haul, no matter how resilient you are. At some point, the chances are you'll decide life's too short for all that misery, and default back to your previous, more comfortable ways.

The final, and perhaps most important, reason willpower alone won't sustain your success is the problem of *distraction*.

When you are driving hard,
you are working against yourself.

Part of you wants to take the aligned action because you want the results, but part of you wants something else even more. Your desire to do whatever it takes to reach your goal bumps up against your natural desire to feel free, live fully and enjoy the moment. These apparently competing intentions require you to be consciously vigilant, continually overriding the impulse to do something else – something easier, more comfortable, more fun. And that means the moment you are distracted and your headspace is taken up with other things, your autopilot will kick in and you will default back to habit. It's perfectly possible to debug your autopilot programming, and harness its power in *support* of your goals, so you can make progress consistently, enjoyably and relatively effortlessly: more on that in Chapter 12. But this can only happen if you work *with* yourself, not against yourself.

When you recognise that *all your desires are valid*, you can begin to find ways to meet all your needs – strategies for getting to where you want to be and loving the journey.

If you have big things you want to achieve and contribute at work, and in your life as a whole, willpower alone can get you started but it won't keep you going. If you grind to a halt, it's not your fault. The on-again/off-again motivation you may have experienced in the past is the inevitable result of driving hard.

Fire up your thrill power!

So, if not willpower, then what *is* the basis of authentic, enjoyable, sustainable success? It's time to shift from desperation to *inspiration*.

It's time to ditch the willpower and switch to *thrill* power!

Whether desperation gets you started and the shift to inspiration is gradual, or you're inspired from the start, what transforms your experience of the journey is maintaining your focus on what you truly and authentically want for yourself. Shifting your attention between a future vision of the new and improved life circumstances you intend to create and noticing everything in your life right now that already matches your dream destination. Loving where you are, and where you're going.

As you envision your dream destination, anything unwanted in your current situation is just a snapshot in time, a 'before' picture that will one day mark the incredible progress you've made. As you shift your focus to your dream destination, excited and curious to discover what's possible for you, every move you make feels like a chance to make progress. You feel good about making authentic choices and taking aligned action. In addition to any progress you make against whatever metrics first prompted you to commit, you begin to notice all the many additional benefits of the changes you have made. You are pleasantly surprised by these unanticipated bonuses, and every time you notice something new, you feel even more inspired to continue. Even apparent setbacks teach you something new about the terrain you are navigating and how to make progress, and you incorporate those discoveries in support of even greater success. Measurable progress causes your motivation to increase as you move consistently closer to your dream destination.

Even more importantly, because you're not firing yourself up by making where you are 'wrong', you're able to enjoy your life as it is right now.

Your relaxed and inspired state allows your brain and nervous system to operate optimally, making new connections and serving up ideas and inspirations you'd miss if you were stressed.

You connect easily with others who can support you, and you feel safe enough to ask for help. You recognise that your point of power is always here and now, and you capitalise on every opportunity to make forward progress.

And as you continue to keep your authentic commitment, you appreciate yourself even more and your self-confidence grows. As you approach your original dream destination, you can see beyond to a new horizon that beckons you. As you celebrate each magical milestone, a new and even more vibrant dream destination calls you forward. You feel deeply satisfied with where you are right now *and* ready for even more. You're driving for big results and loving the journey!

Now, imagine living your *whole life* that way. Imagine the impact of shifting from an over-reliance on *desperation* to a life fuelled by *inspiration*. Imagine achieving extraordinary results, only rarely needing to rely on willpower, energised instead by authentic *thrill power*.

In the corporate world, with its focus on here-and-now performance and productivity, it's considered a great compliment to be described simply as 'driven'. But driven by what? I invite you to make a crucial, potentially life-changing distinction. Because if you want to do your best work, make your most significant and authentic contribution and have your action feel enjoyable and sustainable for the long haul, being driven by fear won't cut it.

Breaking free from driving hard

Is an inspired and joyful journey compatible with dedication to a demanding, high-achieving career? And if so, what might such an inspired life's work look, sound and feel like?

To envision this, let's begin by remembering that, while the journey from where you are to where you want to be may be linear – from past to present to future – the way you travel naturally *cycles through active and inactive phases*. As we've already explored, when you take a long-distance road trip, progress is made in stages: churning up the miles for a while, then pulling over for a break.

The rest stops are a necessary change of pace, as essential to the journey as the driving itself.

On a long-distance trip, you stop and start several times, shifting between forward progress and restful reorientation with full awareness of the importance of both. But whether you relish your rest stops or resent them – wishing you could just press on and 'get there' faster – depends on what's driving you. Fear and love can each drive both action and inaction in a complete and self-sustaining pattern of behaviour that becomes habit over time. But the underlying direction of motivation – away from what you don't want or towards what you do want – drives two very different experiences.

Fear mode demands hard driving.
Love mode allows authentic thriving.

Credit for my own recognition of these two different ways of experiencing life goes to author and teacher Gill Edwards. Back in 2008, when I first met Gill, my work was already keenly focused on the idea of 'effortless success'. For many years, I had been reading widely and reflecting deeply on how we can strip out the struggle and drive for our authentic dreams. I wanted to fully understand what helps and what hinders us in recognising and then engaging with our most significant life's work, and in experiencing joy along the way: getting there and loving here. I had come to recognise the powerful underlying forces of fear and love, and the two ways of being and doing that they created, and I was speaking publicly about the difference between 'driving hard' and what I then called 'driving on cruise control'. But it was only on reading Gill's beautiful book *Pure Bliss* (2009) that I understood the cyclical nature of these two ways of being. It is with thanks to her for this crucial distinction that I share with you the following insights, and distinctions I've made ever since.

Like the physical road trip described above, this metaphorical journey – your career, your life – includes both active and inactive phases, bursts of forward progress followed by moments where you slow down to rest, reflect and reset your direction. Each tiny cycle that makes up your day is nested within larger cycles that represent your days, weeks, months and years of overall forward progress. On a micro level this might take the form of a brief period of focused productivity, followed by stretching your legs and grabbing a coffee before choosing your next priority action and diving back in. These small cycles run for an hour or two and sit nestled within the larger cycle of your day, with the working day ideally offset by a change of pace in the evening. If the rhythm of your work fits with standard office hours, then these daily cycles sit within a weekly cycle of workdays and weekends. These weekly cycles sit within cycles that are longer still – a pattern of months of work punctuated by a week or two of leave. Each cycle features both an active and a more passive stage, with the active phase focused on forward motion and the passive phase earmarked for rest and recovery, reflection and planning, and – at least in theory – genuine fun, connection and rejuvenation.

As we have already explored, you know you're driving hard when you are focused on *surviving*. You may dream of someday truly *thriving* – of somehow getting on top of everything that needs to be done – so that you can find time to create and contribute your best work *and* rest, reflect and relish your life. But if you're driving hard, your day-to-day experience is one of pushing as hard and as fast as possible to get through everything that *must* be done, driven by the fear that you might miss deadlines, squander opportunities or let other people down.

This level of chronic hard driving takes its toll, particularly if you also have significant caring responsibilities outside work, such as raising children or supporting elderly relatives. As we've already explored, driving hard draws relentlessly on your willpower, which is a finite resource. Once it runs out, you grind to a halt.

This is the shift from willpower to '*nil power*'.

When you slow down or stop because you're exhausted and feel you have no choice, rest is often fitful and far from restorative. Even time marked out for fun and friendship may be tainted with persistent and intrusive negative thoughts as you compulsively revisit the day's events and anxiously anticipate or rage against whatever lies ahead. This can lead to a reliance on activities that help us to wind down by numbing these uncomfortable thoughts and feelings – food, alcohol, endless scrolling. At first, these distractions are pleasant and bring a feeling of relief. But over time they become part of the problem, contributing to your exhaustion and frustration.

If this hard-driving cycle (Fig. 3.1) plays out over an extended period, you may begin to recognise the telltale signs that you're on the road to burnout – mental fog, trouble focusing, difficulty sleeping, fluctuating appetite, chronic anxiety and irritability.

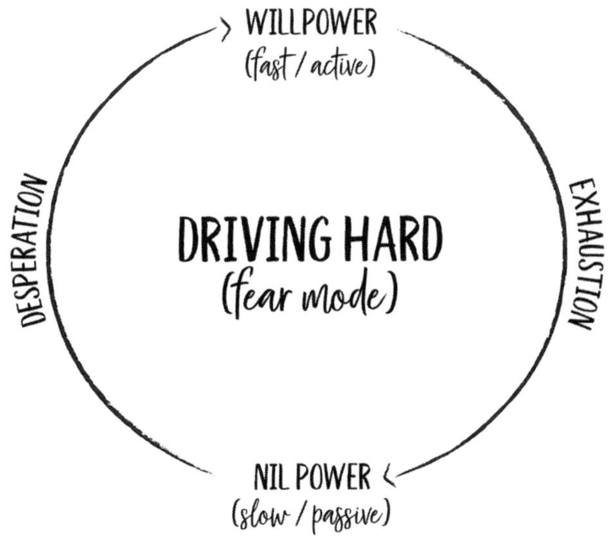

Fig. 3.1: Driving Hard – the Willpower / Nil Power Cycle

Eventually your fear of the consequences if you slow down is outweighed by your fear of the consequences if you don't.

This decision to slow down may be temporary, such as taking a holiday because you need a break or because you've hardly seen family or friends. Or it may be longer term, such as lowering your career ambitions in line with what feels more realistic from this chronically exhausted and dissatisfied state. Either way, the rewards of shifting from willpower to nil power are rarely as great as we hope they will be. And if you dilute your dreams in an attempt to protect yourself from disappointment, your disappointment is almost guaranteed. Your own untapped and unrealised potential weighs heavier than you ever imagined it would. You know that there must be more to life than this. But, locked in a fear-driven loop, shifting between willpower and nil power, it may seem as though you have little choice but to settle for far less than you truly desire. But thankfully you do have a choice.

From driving hard to driving happy

There is an alternative to the willpower/nil power cycle of driving hard, one that enables you to pursue your dreams in a way that is enjoyable, expansive and even more effective. It's the shift that makes the difference between driving hard and driving happy.

When you're authentically *inspired* towards your dream destination, little if any willpower is required to get you started. In almost the same moment that the idea arises – an inspired action that could move you towards your authentic goal – the energy also arises to take that action.

You know this from your own experience. Think of a time when you heard that tickets were about to go on sale for an event you were excited to attend – the chance to see your favourite band or to join the crowd at a pivotal sports match. Did you have to dig deep into your willpower to log on to the agent's website and book your ticket? Of course not!

You didn't need willpower because you had *thrill power*.

So it is in your career and life as a whole. If you trust your intuitive impulses and swiftly move to *take inspired action*, you can ride that natural wave of energy through to the completion of the task. You can get great results and have fun along the way.

As this wave of thrill power naturally dissipates, it is replaced by a calm and contented stillness, a moment of contemplation, reflection or celebration.

This is *still power*, an expansive state – open minded and open hearted – that allows you to connect on a deeper level with who *you really* are, and creates space for the next inspired action to become clear.

Moment by moment, day by day, still power triggers thrill power and thrill power gives way to still power in a virtuous cycle of calm reflection and inspired action (Fig. 3.2).

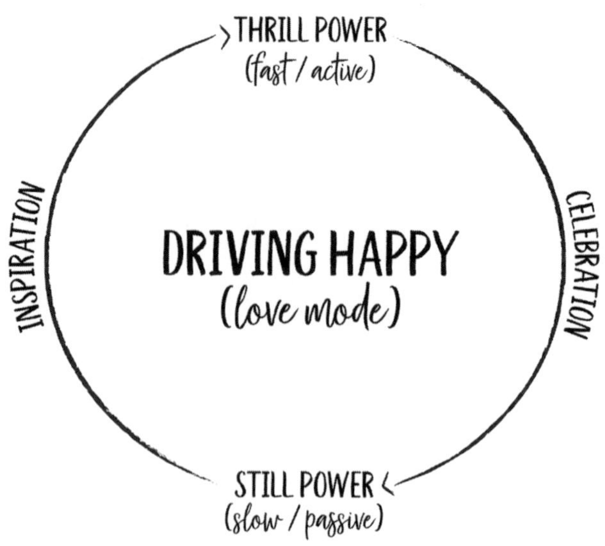

Fig. 3.2: Driving Happy – the Thrill Power / Still Power Cycle

Shifting from driving hard to driving happy is an extraordinary experience, and you can feel the difference immediately (Fig. 3.3). It's almost as though you have slipped into a parallel universe, one in which work often feels like play, and 'fitting in' gives way to a true sense of belonging. Embracing your inspired ideas, and riding the authentic energy that arises when you do, creates an ongoing sense of ease and flow. Momentum builds and, before you know it, you're making progress at speed in a way that really does feel like driving on cruise control. Yes, you still need to steer, but everything else happens automatically – true effortless success.

I've shared this idea often enough with audiences and coaching clients by now to expect a degree of scepticism. After all, you are an intelligent, capable person, and if it was that simple, you'd have figured it out by now, right?

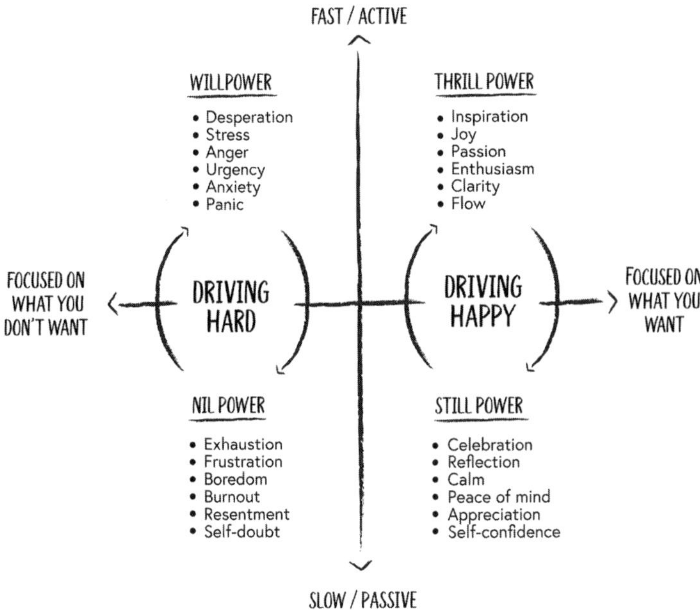

Fig. 3.3: Emotional Indicators of Driving Hard vs Driving Happy

But this is not a matter of intelligence. Rather it's a matter of recognising the years, perhaps even decades, of conditioning telling you to mistrust your own impulses, ignore your body's signals and drive hard for results at almost any cost.

Creating a career and life that you love requires that you strip back any such conditioning that no longer serves you, or that was never you in the first place. It involves rediscovering the deeper knowing and authentic desires you were trained away from, re-learning to trust *yourself* first and foremost. That begins with paying a little less attention to the strategies, opinions and limiting assumptions of others, and a little more attention to your own inner guidance. It's about clawing back some of the time you've been spending with your attention fixated on the outside world and settling into an exploration of your rich inner world. It's about taking back the personal power you've unwittingly given to others, reclaiming your journey as your own.

It's about moving forward at speed by first coming home to yourself.

In later chapters we'll look much more closely at how to cultivate still power as a superpower, so you can discover your *inner* zone of genius and envision your *outer* dream destination – an accomplishment and contribution unique to you, one truly worthy of your time, energy and talents. We'll leverage thrill power so that you can optimise your journey, build momentum and achieve astonishing results – all with your health, relationships and sanity intact. And we'll achieve this by examining three key areas:

1. **Mindset** – How to challenge the assumptions, beliefs and paradigms that trap you in driving hard, and replace them with more empowering beliefs and perspectives that align you with driving happy.
2. **Heartset** – How to tap into your own deep wisdom and authentic values and inspire yourself towards joyful and meaningful contribution.
3. **Skillset** – How to cultivate the skills and core capabilities that enable you to harness the power of momentum and make progress like a pro.

Let's begin by looking at the key skill that you'll need to practise if you're going to make the shift from driving hard to driving happy. The shift from focusing on what you *don't* want to focusing on what you *do* want. The shift out of fear mode and back into love mode. The shift from barely surviving to truly thriving.

4. From Surviving to Thriving

When it comes to any kind of psychological fear, the 'feel' is real, but the 'why' is a lie.

– Guy Finley, The Secret of Letting Go (2007)
American author and spiritual teacher

Warning: adverse camber ahead!

In my early days as a learner driver, I caught sight of a sign I did not understand. It read 'Warning: adverse camber ahead!' I looked to my instructor for an explanation. 'It means there's a slope on the road, from one side to the other,' he explained. 'If you grip the wheel loosely, you'll naturally veer into oncoming traffic. You have to actively steer into the slope, just to drive straight.'

As on the road, so in life. Making the shift from fear to love is not a one-time decision. There is an 'adverse camber' on the road in the direction of fear, a tendency to overemphasise the risks and undervalue the opportunity in any situation. This tendency is both fast and completely automatic. You have probably experienced for yourself how quickly any fear-based thinking can gain momentum. One troubling thought triggers the next and the next, and before you know it, you're running a full-blown disaster movie in your head.

Unless you train yourself to compensate for this tendency by steering your attention towards love and appreciation, your thinking will naturally veer towards fear.

This automatic tendency is known as the negativity bias, and it is rooted both in nurture and nature. First, the negativity bias is 'soft-wired' into your system, for reasons we've already explored: the training you received as a learner driver. Conditioning over time has literally shaped your brain and primed your nervous system to overestimate risk and undervalue opportunity. This bias is not limited to those who have lived through the trauma of adverse childhood experiences. Even the most well intentioned of parents, carers and teachers want their young charges to comply with the expectations and judgements of others, to follow the rules and fit in, in the hope they will be protected and get along in life. So, even if you were fortunate enough to also receive many messages of support and encouragement, the overall balance was almost certainly in favour of *safety* rather than authenticity, adventure and growth. The chances are those early voices have been internalised as 'back seat drivers' in your head, still cautioning you today. You may regularly remind yourself to hold back and play it safe, without even recognising consciously that *the voice in your head is not your own.*

You're hard-wired to survive

The second and more enduring reason for the negativity bias is the fundamental wiring of your human brain and nervous system. Our hunter-gatherer ancestors only made it through the day in one piece if they spotted threats and survived them. The ones who heard a rustling sound in a nearby bush and assumed it was 'just the breeze' are the ones who didn't last long enough to pass on their DNA! You and I are the direct descendants of the early humans who were the quickest to recognise potential threats, the ones who – in moments of uncertainty – assumed the worst and shifted into fear-based 'fight or flight'.

Your incredible mind–body vehicle was brand new on the day you were born, but it was built to an ancient design – one more suited to a verdant jungle than a concrete one.

You are hard wired for survival. It's in your DNA. Committing to compensate for the adverse camber by steering into love mode will not make you blind to the risk. Rather, it will allow you the genuine best chance to handle any challenges intelligently and in a way that serves you both now and in the long run.

What's more, steering into the positives buffers you against sudden and unexpected hard times. Your journey won't always be easy. There will be times when life will challenge you to your core. The promise of committing and re-committing to loving the journey is that in such challenging moments you will have retrained yourself to see opportunities where others see only problems. And if you are seriously triggered into fear and find yourself nose down in a ditch, you'll find your way back out again faster and with relative ease.

Even in moments when 'effortless success' is not possible, you will be ready and able to 'effort' less.

Accepting that there will be challenging times ahead gives us even more reason to ensure that we can work through and release stress and anxiety, so that all the energy we invest in the journey goes into creating the results and experiences we want.

It's important to understand that the fearful part of you that takes charge when you are triggered by a perceived threat is *not* intentionally sabotaging your progress. You are not being 'your own worst enemy'. You do not have inner demons that need to be slain.

This risk-averse and ever-vigilant part of you is your *inner protector*.

This is the aspect of your unconscious mind charged with ensuring you continue to exist. It has a job to do, and it uses the fear circuitry of your brain and nervous system to do it. And it believes quite literally that your life depends on it doing that job well.

Make friends with your inner protector

Your inner protector is an aspect of your personality, a cluster of beliefs, values and automatic strategies. It is constantly running in the background and scanning your environment for threats and problems. And it is hell-bent on keeping you safe at any cost.

Have you ever been driving along, relaxed and enjoying the ride, only to instantaneously come to full attention due to a flicker of movement in the corner of your eye? The fear circuitry of your brain assesses the situation and almost immediately shifts your foot from the accelerator to the brake, preparing your whole body to execute an emergency stop. In a tiny fraction of a second, your unconscious mind uses the fast tracks in your brain to compare the image to a plethora of other known shapes and patterns of movement. Is it a dog? A cat? A child on a bike? Your inner protector finds a match – a plastic bag swirling in the breeze – and signals the 'all clear'. You are safe, for now. You drive on, breathing deep and slow to help clear the adrenaline.

Your ever-vigilant inner protector craves certainty in an uncertain world. It nudges you to play it safe by sticking with what you know.

Familiarity and prior experience make it easier to predict and control what will happen next. And in moments of uncertainty, in the absence of actual facts, your inner protector fills in the gaps with worst-case assumptions.

If you choose to override these mental disaster movies – venturing out into unfamiliar territory filled with new people, new circumstances and first-time attempts at new activities – your inner protector will be on high alert, hyper-vigilant for threats and ready to take control of the wheel in a fraction of a second.

At best, an overactive inner protector can suck the fun out of what could otherwise be thrilling new experiences. At worst, it can stop you venturing outside your comfort zone in the first place, resulting in you living a far smaller life than the one you want and deserve – the one that would most benefit you, your loved ones and the world at large. When we mentally rehearse disaster, we stress ourselves out – even when things are going well. As Mark Twain famously said, 'I am an old man, and have known a great many troubles, most of which never happened.'

Make space for your inner adventurer

But merely existing and fully living are two very different experiences. Thankfully, your mind–body vehicle isn't solely wired for safety. It is also wired for exploration, discovery and *pleasure*. After all, if our fearful hunter-gatherer ancestors had stayed hidden away, they'd have starved to death. Your brain and nervous system are also hard wired to reach for benefits and rewards, and to reinforce the choices that led to your discoveries with a feel-good dose of dopamine. This 'pleasure circuitry', if leveraged with love for yourself and others rather than rampant consumption, supports your inner adventurer, the part of you that actively seeks out new and different experiences.

Your inner adventurer is opportunity focused, craving stimulation, discovery and growth. It imagines the 'more' that is possible, and takes action to find, create and experience that new and improved condition. Your inner adventurer is creative and innovative, thinks big and delights in taking inspired action.

The ability to imagine and anticipate the future, and take decisive action here and now to shape our world towards that vision, is the reason that humans are the dominant species on our planet. It's important to remember, as explored in Chapter 1, that this pleasure circuitry can be hijacked if your underlying motivation is still the avoidance of what you don't want. Self-destructive and addictive behaviours all light up the pleasure circuitry and yet are all rooted in scarcity and fear. Fear reduces you from the powerful creator you were born to be to the insatiable consumer of other people's creations. So, it's important to recognise that driving a mind–body vehicle that came factory fitted with the pleasure circuitry that drives your inner adventurer does not in itself guarantee you a thrilling ride, particularly in the long haul.

You are hard wired to survive, but only soft wired with the potential to truly thrive.

You cannot tap this incredible potential to thrive if the actions you take are still driven by fearful thinking. Only when your actions are driven by loving intentions – the desire to create or contribute something new and different, which is good for the group as well as yourself – are you on track to truly love the journey.

It's crucial to listen to your inner protector. It has an important role to play in ensuring you live long enough to reach your dreams. But instead of acquiescing to or overriding any stressful thoughts, you can identify and release your fear-based thinking and put measures in place to manage and mitigate any genuine risks. You can recognise that staying right where you are, doing more of what you're already doing also carries significant risk. And when you acknowledge the risks inherent in playing small, it's easier to get your inner protector on board with a new, more adventurous, more authentic course of action. You can begin to steer your imagination towards what you really *want* for yourself, your loved ones and the world at large.

That's when you shift back from consumer to creator. That's when you discover your most authentic dream destination, the unique and wondrous life your inner protector and inner adventurer can help you create – if you get them working together. That's what will allow you to drive for your dreams *and* thrive as you drive.

Selectively sift your scenery

How do you shift from being driven by fear to being driven by love? In this moment, the answer is simple: find something you love and give it your attention. You don't have to wait until you reach your dream destination. You don't have to wait even a moment longer. Just start where you are.

Joy happens in any moment where you give your undivided attention to someone or something you love. Happiness happens when you give your *sustained* attention to who and what you love.

Try it now.

- Scan your environment for something beautiful.
- Give your attention to the best qualities in the people around you.
- Think of something you're looking forward to and relish the anticipation.

Notice how you feel. And imagine what your life would be like if you could maintain this focus more of the time.

Simple, right? But simple doesn't necessarily mean easy. Why? Because, as we've already explored, decades of 'learner driver' training conditioned you to remain vigilant, to scan where you are now for anything that is wrong or inadequate in some way. Otherwise, so the conditioned story goes, you will become complacent and demotivated, and you won't take action to make progress and improve your situation. So, when you give your attention to something you love, the chances are your thoughts will soon turn to something you don't. You may enjoy a moment of appreciation for your home, then find yourself noticing your limited space or feeling the weight of your mortgage or the strain of making the rent. You may appreciate your partner, but then shift to their most irritating habit or how stressed your relationship feels at times. You may appreciate your job, then find yourself annoyed by your commute or by that one person who picks holes in everything you do.

So, if happiness happens when you give *sustained attention to things you love*, but your inner protector is constantly pulling your attention back to everything that is not as it should be, how can you make the shift from fear to love stick for the long haul? How can you come home to the real you, who you really are underneath all that conditioning?

Find your authentic homing beacon

Before you can *shift* your thinking, you must become aware of your thinking. You have to pull back far enough to see that you are not your thoughts, but the one thinking, the one observing those thoughts.

**The voice in your head is not you:
you are the one who is
listening to that voice.**

Adopting this 'observer' position creates some separation, a little distance, perspective. Instead of constantly reacting to the continuous stream of thoughts – the good, the bad and the ugly – as the mindful observer of your thoughts, you can rediscover and reintroduce choice. You have the chance to examine the stories running in your head, to explore their basis and to question their truth. And as you do, you begin to recognise a profoundly important truth:

Thoughts that are in harmony with *who you really are* feel harmonious in your body.

Every experience you have can show you something about who you are and who you are not. Every moment contains both wanted and unwanted features, things you love and things you don't. As you practise tuning yourself to your genuine preferences and desires, the world becomes a mirror for your most authentic self. You become far more aware, and far more discerning about what is true for you, and what is just a convincing falsehood.

You gain control over your thoughts, rather than your thoughts having control over you.

This work is never 'done'. But the good news is that every time you recognise even one fear-based thought and replace it with a thought that feels kinder and more harmonious inside you, you're making progress. And you are rewarded for that instantaneously. You rendezvous with who you really are and align with a life that you love, not at some point off in the distant future, but right here, right now.

Shifting from fear to love always feels like relief, and often feels like pure joy. This feeling of harmony and alignment is your authentic homing beacon, guiding you to the truth of who you really are. You will feel the shift every time you refocus, from 'How can I change this unwanted situation?' to 'How can I create what I want instead?'

Check this out for yourself. Bring to mind a small event from your day that you would have preferred to avoid, something that you found moderately stressful. Now get curious. Look closer and see what you can find to appreciate in the situation, by completing the sentence, '__________ happened, and that's a good thing because ____________.' See if you can recognise the skills you had the chance to hone (conflict resolution, focus, holding clear boundaries, etc.) and the personal qualities you had the chance to develop (patience, compassion, courage, etc.). Your inner protector will still point out the risks to be managed and any improvements to be made. This is simply a chance to ensure your thinking is well rounded. And to feel yourself shift from your stress response into a relaxation response.

Practise the shift

Over time and with practice you'll become more sensitive to fear-based thoughts as they arise. You'll notice them more quickly and question them automatically. This in turn will allow you to progressively leave behind old 'truths' – fear-driven beliefs you picked up from others along your trail – and discover what is *true for you*.

I stepped out into my garden this morning to find Mother Nature had put on a spectacular display. Fiery flashes of crimson and gold across an indigo sky. It was breathtakingly beautiful. I snapped a quick pic to share later with my sleeping family, then stood for a further five minutes, fully present to the experience. My pleasure circuitry lit up as I allowed the beauty and vibrancy of the sky to fill my heart, sink into my bones and infuse every cell of my being.

The impact of recognising and allowing blissful moments such as this goes far beyond relieving any stress you may have been feeling. Over time the effect is cumulative, counteracting the built-in negativity bias and physically rewiring your brain in the direction of positive experiences.

This is the master shift, the shift from fear to love, from merely surviving to truly thriving. At first, this takes a certain amount of focus, as your habitual ways of thinking, doing and being have significant momentum. Thankfully, there are many ways we can make this transition quicker, easier and more enjoyable. In Chapters 12 and 13 we'll look in depth at how you can *activate your autopilot* and debug any outdated or glitchy programming, so you can get the gravitational pull of habit working in your favour. But if you're willing to play with this shift 'in manual' for a while, you can begin to benefit immediately from momentum in your new chosen direction.

Every time you deliberately refocus your attention in the direction of what you do want, you are retraining your mind to do the same – automatically, effortlessly and in ways that will endlessly surprise and delight you.

You can begin to experience a life you love by noticing what you love about the life you're already living.

And as you relax into focusing on what you most genuinely and uniquely want to create, contribute and experience, you transform the relentless race into a truly authentic adventure.

5. Adventures in the Courage Zone

I'm always doing things I can't do.
That's how I get to do them.

– Pablo Picasso
20th century Spanish artist, prolifically inventive co-founder of Cubism

The call to adventure

A young man on a desert-covered planet joins his uncle's search for a suitable droid. And so we catch our first glimpse of Luke Skywalker, the unlikely hero of George Lucas's epic sci-fi saga, *Star Wars*. As potential heroes go, he's not a promising candidate. Certainly, we soon discover that he is bright, skilful and technically resourceful. But we also hear him whine and complain almost incessantly as he goes about his familiar and mundane tasks.

Over dinner, he asks his uncle about their 'agreement' – the expectation that Luke will stay on at the family farm for another year – and expresses his wish to instead replace himself with more droids and head off to The Academy. But, with the harvest looming, he is reminded that he is needed right where he is. There is work to do – important work – and his uncle assures him it's for 'just one more season'. As he steps away from the dinner table, Luke mumbles under his breath, 'That's what you said last year...'

So, we follow our young protagonist outside and, in one of the most iconic movie scenes of all time, see him gaze across the desert at a binary sunset and resign himself to yet another year of life on Tatooine, the planet farthest from the bright centre of the galaxy.

Luke Skywalker is a compelling character because we meet him on the brink of an authentic adventure. He's feeling life call him towards more. And whether or not you are a member of the Star Wars fandom that has endured for four decades, the appeal of that one iconic scene is almost universal. Why? Because life is constantly calling *us all* towards our own authentic adventure.

If you made it this far, you too are feeling the call to adventure – even if it has come in the form of 'enough is enough'. But if you've been driving hard for success using the well-intentioned, but fundamentally flawed, route map to success you were given, you may not be feeling particularly 'heroic' right now. You may have been on the receiving end of experiences and feedback that caused you to doubt yourself and your abilities. You may even have come to doubt that you are truly worthy of the success and happiness you desire. None of that matters, because you can *decide* today that the old rules of the road no longer apply. Whether you are underwhelmed or overwhelmed by life as it is, your journey can be experienced very differently from here, by answering that call to authentic adventure.

You are being called to more – a more joyful experience of work and life, lived by a more joyful and even more resourceful version of you.

Choosing comfort over chaos

So why might you hesitate to embrace life as an authentic adventure? The answer, of course, is fear.

As we have already explored in Chapter 3, fear is a powerful driving force that can motivate you to action. But as we found in Chapter 4, it is also a force that can hold you back. As much as you feel the resonance with the heroes of your favourite novels, Hollywood blockbusters and even the real-life stories of the greatest leaders of our time, you've also seen the extremes of their journeys – the trials and tribulations experienced along the way, often involving extreme threat to life and limb. You see the chaos that can arise from stepping away from the well-worn path of conformity and compliance. It's rare to see on the big screen the stories of the countless real-life heroes – people like you and me – who are following their dreams, embracing uncertainty, collaborating and contributing, overcoming adversity and along the way becoming who they were born to be. The big screen is reserved only for those who've earned superhero status. And the impression that can create is that the choice you face when adventure calls is between the relative comfort of sticking with what you know versus the potential chaos of whatever might be waiting for you out there in the bigger, more rewarding, more you-shaped world beyond.

Faced with an apparent choice between comfort and chaos, the safest course of action seems absolutely clear, and your inner protector will work hard to keep you right where you are. 'Get your head out of the clouds. Play it safe. Do enough to make sure you deliver in your current role, but don't risk over-reaching. In fact, don't take risks at all if you can avoid it. Get your kicks from the entertainment industry, or from intense and immersive role-playing games, where you can be a hero from the comfort of your armchair. After all, you don't want to do anything to jeopardise the life you've built for yourself, or that might drive a wedge between you and your loved ones, your friendship group and the network of peers and seniors that you've so carefully curated so far....'

But the choice between comfort and chaos is not the true choice before you. You already know what happens when you don't take care of what matters most to you when those things are merely *important*. Eventually those important things – your health, your self-esteem, your wellbeing, your personal growth, your authentic relationships – become *urgent*. And when something that is deeply important to you becomes urgent, that's what we call a *crisis*. Instead of the challenging-*and-thrilling* experience of taking inspired and authentic action, you're thrown into the chaos of a crisis. And as you wrestle with the wheel trying to regain control, conditions are ripe for you to slide off into a ditch. If you continue to refuse the call towards growth and authentic contribution, you may find yourself navigating a prolonged 'rough patch' where it seems you're lurching from one crisis to another with barely a moment to catch your breath. *Inauthenticity is exhausting!*

When your comfort zone gets uncomfortable

Thankfully, there is a space in between comfort and chaos, and it's the space where real-life heroes hang out.

Between your comfort zone and the chaos zone lies your courage zone.

To understand your courage zone – what it is, how to get there and how to stay there – let's first take a closer look at your comfort zone.

In every moment you are simultaneously navigating not one but two journeys: the *outer* journey of people, places and things, and your own *inner* journey of thoughts, sensations and emotions. If you use the term 'comfort zone' in the way that it is used by most people, then you're most likely describing your outer world – a set of circumstances that is so familiar to you that you can predict what's likely to happen next. This familiarity allows you to draw on your experience, which leads in turn to the feeling of comfort: relaxed, at peace and reasonably confident that 'whatever happens next, I'll handle it'. And therein lies the crunch.

If feeling safe and self-confident depends on your ability to predict and control what will happen next, then you have to create a very limited world for yourself.

In an attempt to manage the inherent uncertainties of everyday life, you may become hyper-vigilant for threats and resistant to change, anxiously acknowledging that it's simply not possible to predict and control the world. Even if you make your world small enough to be manageable, what once felt comfortably familiar soon becomes uncomfortably dull and repetitive. As you diligently stay away from the uncomfortable edge of this 'familiarity zone' – sticking with what you know and allowing your ability to learn, grow and develop to atrophy – you eventually find yourself on an inner journey that is anything but comfortable. You were built for growth, not for driving round and round in the same old circles. What's more, if there's a major disturbance in your environment that makes it extremely difficult to predict and control even within this small life you're allowing yourself – a health challenge, threats of redundancy, a global pandemic – your confidence is swept away because the story in your head flips to 'I don't know what to do. I don't feel safe. I'm not sure I can handle this!' And either gradually or suddenly your chronic low-grade stress can bloom into full-blown panic.

Sacrificing your dreams does not protect you from the chaos zone.

So how can you access that space in between? How can you embrace your call to adventure?

The zone between comfort and chaos

Let's look again at your comfort zone, and this time make a new distinction – one that will allow you to feel comfortable under a far wider range of conditions, and enable you to move forward with authentic joy. Your 'familiarity zone' – the predictable outer circumstances you believed you needed to feel comfortable and confident – were not actually what generated that state. Rather it was *what you said to yourself* in response to those circumstances. 'I've got this.' So, when it comes to accessing your inner state of ease, comfort and confidence, your self-talk matters more than your situation. Your comfort zone is the combination of familiar circumstances and encouraging self-talk:

'I can do this! And whatever happens next, I'll handle it.'

Now, let's look again at the chaos zone. It is an unfamiliar and unpredictable set of circumstances combined with unsupportive and discouraging self-talk: 'I don't know what's happening. I can't do this!' (see Fig. 5.1)

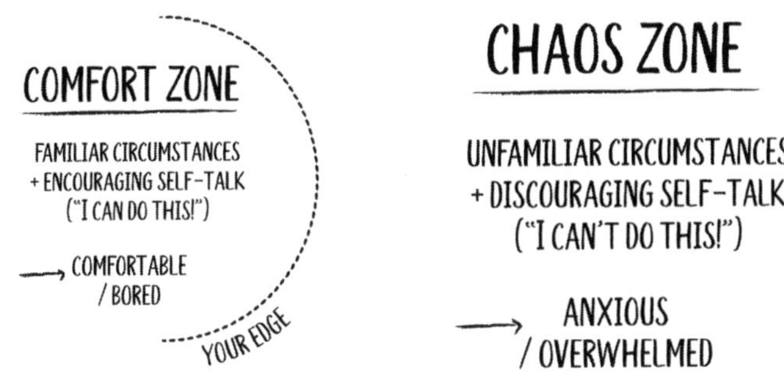

Fig. 5.1: Your Comfort Zone vs the Chaos Zone

Recognising this distinction gives you access to your courage zone (see Fig. 5.2). And that's because encouraging self-talk – the most essential aspect of your comfort zone – is totally *portable*. You can take it with you wherever you go. Even in unfamiliar and unpredictable territory, you can remind yourself that you are already capable and readily able to learn even more.

You access the courage zone by encouraging yourself.

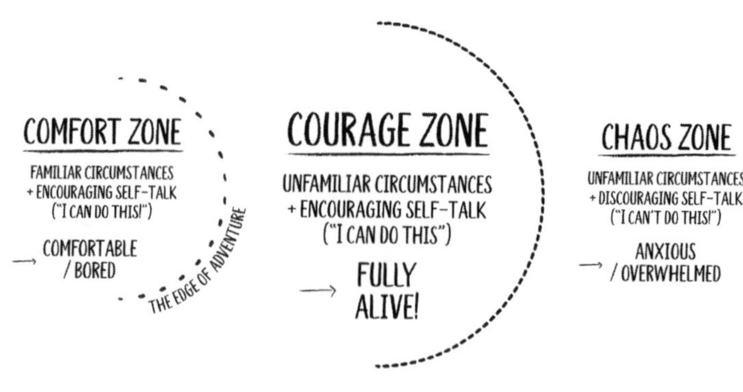

Fig. 5.2: Finding Your Courage Zone

Are you facing something challenging right now, something that will require courage to navigate? Whether it's a major roadblock or a wonderful but somewhat overwhelming new opportunity, imagine it was your best friend or a brilliant colleague who was in your place. What would you say to support and encourage them? Now say that to yourself.

Instead of trusting in your ability to predict and control your outer world, shift your attention inward and cultivate *trust in yourself*: 'Whatever happens next, I'll handle it.'

And you have every reason to trust yourself in this way, regardless of any well-worn story that may suggest otherwise. After all, you have a 100 per cent track record of handling everything that's come your way so far. It may not always have been pretty, and it may at times have been extraordinarily painful. I know from my own experience that the chaos zone can chew you up and spit you out (some of what I've dealt with has been handled through a veil of tears and snot bubbles!). But you're still here, and you handled it all. Understanding that the distress of the chaos zone was driven by your self-talk – the story that you were telling yourself rather than the situation you were in – creates a new opportunity for a very different experience if you ever encounter such a major challenge again.

When you commit to becoming more and more mindful of how you talk to yourself, as well as more and more discerning about the comments you let in from others, courage and *authentic self-confidence* can be yours. You create a safe space on the inside from which to effectively handle whatever happens on the outside. And with that, you cultivate the ability to be who you really are under an ever-expanding range of circumstances.

You know where you are and where you want to be. Embracing the uncertainty of the journey in between – recognising that you don't know, *can't know*, everything that will happen along the way – is the very thing that transforms the journey into a lifelong adventure.

True self-confidence comes as a by-product of doing things you're not absolutely certain you can do.

So, stretch yourself just a little, every single day. Meet life exactly as it shows up. Bring your best self to the moment, to the best of your ability, and discover even more about who you really are underneath that lifetime of conditioning. Yes, you may encounter major roadblocks along the way, but you can back yourself in the moment and access your courage zone with these simple words: 'I can do this. And whatever happens next, I'll handle it.'

The roadblock is the way

And that's the wonderful truth about roadblocks. Though such challenges and obstacles may first seem to be evidence that something has gone wrong, the reality is they play a vital role in creating your authentic adventure. Roadblocks – seemingly unlovable people, situations and circumstances – show you the limits of your ability to find something you love in every moment. It is these internal barriers to loving your life exactly as it shows up – misaligned values, limiting beliefs or an unhelpful world view – that get in the way of you showing up as who you really are and creating the authentic, joyful and deeply meaningful life you have imagined. When you truly appreciate the moment exactly as it is, you connect with the never-ending flow of inspiration, and you see clearly both what's wonderful about where you are and the even more magnificent possibilities available from here. You're in touch with both profound peace and an exhilarating sense of pure potential.

Every roadblock you successfully navigate provides a unique opportunity for true self-discovery. If you lean into the learning available to you once you're on the other side of any moment of crisis and chaos, you'll find that adversity can be a generous teacher. By being willing to ask, 'What does this distress show me I'm ready to see differently?', you open yourself to the transformative effect of your own authentic adventure. Your greatest fears point to your greatest potential for growth. As Roman emperor and Stoic philosopher Marcus Aurelius observed almost 2,000 years ago:

'What stands in the way becomes the way.'

Look again at the roadblock you identified moments ago (on page 72). Steady yourself still further by pulling back to a broader perspective on your situation and ask, 'What's everything else in my life that's **not** this problem?'

When we're afraid, angry or overwhelmed, we tend to zoom into a close-up of the problem. By pulling back from that fear-induced tunnel vision and expanding your awareness, you are far more likely to maintain your emotional balance. This more resourceful state in turn allows your ideas to flow more easily, and helps maintain your confidence as a resourceful human being: 'I can handle this.'

When you're stuck in the mud, spinning your wheels

How can you recognise and dismantle your *internal* barriers to embracing uncertainty and engaging with life exactly as it shows up, so you can move past any *external* roadblocks to your success and happiness?

Many years ago, I found myself stuck and spinning my wheels – not metaphorically, but quite literally. I'd headed over to a small theme park close to our home to collect my children from an outing with family friends. On finding the main car park full, I followed the hand-painted signs to the overspill parking area – or at least I *thought* I had. I realised I'd gone wrong somewhere when I found myself driving as the only car in an otherwise empty field. I stopped and shifted into a three-point turn, but the car shuddered and my wheels began to spin. I paused, I breathed deeply, and then I held my breath. I pressed the accelerator as gently as possible, hoping for traction, but no... nothing but the shuddering high-pitched 'whir of doom'.

The engine wasn't the only thing over-revving: my mind was whirring too. I couldn't believe I'd made such a stupid mistake. How was I going to get myself out of this mess and, ideally, without anyone else knowing? But this was back in the days before smartphones and Google searches, so my mind was the only search engine available. I grasped for fragments of the Highway Code, snippets of past conversations with my dad, even scenes from movies and television that might hold the secret to getting myself out of this slippery situation. That's when I remembered what I needed to do: wedge something under the wheel for the tyre to grip onto. I grabbed the mat from one of the footwells and gave it my best shot. The result? Nothing but a car mat muddied beyond repair, and tears of frustration.

I took another deep breath, tidied myself up as best I could, and set out on what felt like a long 'walk of shame' to the theme park's welcome desk. The receptionist kindly called for help. A whole team arrived. I mustered a smile, shared my predicament, and played along as they enjoyed a good laugh at my expense. Then I watched in amazement as a small tractor appeared around the corner. In a matter of minutes, my car was free, and so was I. I shouted my thanks but was so keen to escape that I almost drove off without collecting my children!

Learning to love learning

Back home, I cried into an oversized cup of tea. 'I don't understand why it was so stressful,' I sobbed to my husband. 'I know these things happen, but surely I should be able to handle things better? What on earth is *wrong* with me? Why do I have to be so *sensitive*?!'

As my nervous system came down off high alert, my sobbing slowed, and my chastising inner protector gave way to a gentler and wiser presence. I had a sense that this experience was ripe for reflection. If I could let go of my painful story and just see what was actually there, then this *one small experience* would be loaded with insight.

In no time at all I had pages of notes. I saw the choices I'd made and how they'd helped or hindered my progress, and I saw the beliefs at play that drove those choices.

- 'This problem is mine to solve.'
- 'I should know what to do.'
- 'I can't let anyone see I made a mistake.'
- 'Asking for help is mortifying.'

The even more uncomfortable truth was how familiar these thoughts felt to me. Far from being exceptional responses, they were my patterns, and I ran them every time I perceived that I had made a 'stupid mistake'.

In the weeks that followed I committed to a different way of being. I committed to cultivating a kinder, more supportive internal voice in response to challenges. I accepted the invitation of self-compassion expert Dr Kristin Neff to 'be the kindest friend to yourself you are able to be'. And as I did, I learned to play to my strengths without overplaying them, to value my sensitivity as a superpower, to ask for help when I need it, and to keep my most authentic self in the driving seat – even when my fearful ego had other ideas. All from one little experience of getting stuck in the mud.

Get ready for your authentic adventure

It is a potentially life-changing insight to understand that:

- ✦ external roadblocks point to internal barriers of belief
- ✦ it is these internal barriers – not the challenges you encounter along your outer journey – that block your authenticity, connection and joy
- ✦ these internal barriers can be dismantled if you can self-reflect with self-compassion.

Seen in this light, setbacks are not failures but an integral and essential part of your authentic journey. They are a natural occurrence for innovative, aspirational professionals who embrace uncertainty in order to make the biggest possible difference and grow themselves along the way. Knowing this frees you to pour your talents – head, heart and soul – into a truly worthy goal. Assured that you cannot 'lose' – only *learn* – you are better placed to take intelligent, managed risks. You can trust in the goodness of life. You can trust that, whatever happens, you'll handle it.

So, who are *you* really? What gifts are you uniquely positioned to share with the world, your innate zone of genius? What is the dream destination that could inspire you forward with meaning and joy? And what would you most love to create and experience along the way?

It's time to explore and uncover your most authentic adventure.

PART TWO
Your Authentic Adventure

6. Make a You-Turn

What lies behind us and what lies before us are tiny matters compared with what lies within us.

– attributed to Ralph Waldo Emerson
American philosopher and essayist

The race you've already won

Last year, my niece gave birth to a beautiful baby boy. He was the first new arrival in our extended family after a long gap, the first of a whole new generation. It had been a while since I'd held a newborn, but he soon drew me into that old familiar place of pure fascination. How easy it is, as you gaze deep into the eyes of a newborn baby, to know in your bones the preciousness of life.

But, why is that? When you stop to think about it, newborn babies don't *do* anything useful. They cry, they eat, they poop, they sleep. Then the cycle begins again. They make you wait several weeks for so much as a smile. And yet we love them. We *adore* them. We do not expect them to *earn* our affection or approval, to hustle for their worthiness. We already know they are priceless – a living, breathing miracle – worthy simply because they are here.

You were that newborn baby once. And that means that, no matter what you may or may not have achieved so far, your 'worthiness' is not in question. You are worthy beyond measure. The race for worthiness is a race you won by *being born*. You too are a living, breathing miracle, worthy simply because you are here.

If you've lost sight of this foundational truth, it's not surprising. As we've already explored, your introduction to society's rules of the road is likely to have trained you away from a deep and unwavering knowing of your inherent value. Even the kindest, most generous of guidance will have conditioned you to look outside yourself for answers and to mistrust the impulsive and instinctual guidance that came from within.

This socialisation process was crucial at the time. In your early years, it helped you develop foundational life skills such as being able to sit still and pay attention, to be willing to wait for the things you want, and to share what you have with others. But if you're still looking outside yourself for answers as to your best way forward from here, then the patterns set up in those early years to encourage and promote your growth will now be limiting it.

Directions, destinations and discernment

The conditioned pattern of asking other people what you should do is rooted in the equally conditioned belief that there is a 'right way' to do things – including a right way to navigate your career and live your life – and that we should look to others to guide us as to what that right way is. Of course, if you already have a compelling and inspiring vision for your life, then taking direction from others can be a great idea: a caring and insightful mentor can be an extraordinary asset, though it matters a great deal who you ask. For the guidance to be of value to you, it must come from people who are genuinely further along the road you are keen to travel. You wouldn't stop for directions and ask a stranger to choose your actual destination for you, only to ask for guidance as to the most direct or most scenic route to get to where you want to be. And yet your conditioning may open you up to influence by others whose opinions are, quite frankly, of no real relevance to your own unique journey. You may not even consciously recognise the extent to which you listen, let their reactions and opinions in and steer your life accordingly, simply because that's what you were trained to do.

As a tiny child, it took quite a while for the grown-ups around you to get your attention, but they wanted to help you grow and learn so they persevered.

They soon discovered that if they put something you really wanted just out of reach, you would strive to raise yourself up to claim it.

At first it was enough that you tried. When you pulled yourself up on the furniture, it didn't matter that you fell back down. Everyone around you whooped and clapped, soaking up the joy of the moment, with full awareness that falling down is part of the process of learning to stand on your own two feet. You were celebrated for your attempt, for your energy and enthusiasm, for your willingness to give it a go and then keep trying. You were praised for progress, not perfection. But soon thereafter, as your development progressed, results began to count. Comparisons kicked in. Developmental milestones were replaced by standards for your social skills and academic accomplishments. Your achievements were compared against a one-size-fits-all set of expectations of when things should happen. When you met those standards, you were rewarded with approval, and perhaps with praise and affection. When you didn't, unless you're very fortunate, the chances are you weren't.

Over time, the reference point also most likely shifted from an objective set of standards to more subjective expectations based on comparison with your peers, or with any older siblings when they were your age. The expectation may have been set – either openly or implicitly – that you should be 'the best', or at least 'above average', with little if any acknowledgement of the statistical impossibility of everyone being above average.

If you feel like there's something missing...

In this way, countless uniquely joyful journeys are hijacked and turned into a relentless race towards a never-ending stream of standardised milestones. The intention is positive, albeit rooted in a fear-based belief that this is what it takes to get ahead and that 'getting ahead' is what life is all about. But little consideration is given to the beautifully unique and individual journey a young person is born for, the zone of genius they are here to express. The one-size-fits-all approach leaves talents unrecognised, unexplored and undeveloped, and both the individual and the world are poorer for it. As the quote often attributed to Albert Einstein, but actually of unclear origin, says, 'Everyone is a genius. But if you judge a fish by its ability to climb a tree, it will live its whole life believing it is stupid.'

A well-paved career track can help you become the well-rounded and effective professional you would wish to be, but your most authentic adventure will be as individual as you are. If you continue to follow the conditioned rules of the road, endlessly striving towards standardised milestones for success, the chances are your accomplishments will be celebrated by others but feel relatively hollow to you. Having strived and sacrificed to become your 'idealised self' – the person others said you *should* be – there may still be a sense that this is not who you *could* be or *would* be given a free choice. A significant achievement that takes you in the direction of your '*idealised* self' may bring some level of satisfaction, particularly if it meets the needs of others who then heap you with praise and progression. But at some level, you may have a sense that something is missing – in your job, in your relationships, in your life as a whole. And something *is* missing, though it is not anything outside of you.

What is missing from your life is the *real you.*

When you connect more fully to your authentic core – when you allow more of *who you really are* to shine through – your experience of your job, your relationships and your life as a whole is transformed. Feeling like the right person in the right place at the right time is about more than just meeting others' needs in the moment. It's about having a sense that you are doing something that only you can do.

Living your life on purpose is about discovering who you really are, committing to expressing that truest version of yourself in your work and life, and evolving into the person you were born to be.

The journey of true self-discovery

So who are you, really? This is one of the most powerful questions you can ask yourself, and one that must be asked over and over again if your most authentic, joyful and high-contributing life is to be claimed. It's also one of the most challenging to answer.

Life offers you clues in every moment of your journey, but if you weren't taught to recognise the signs, the chances are you won't even see them. You'll simply drive on by in pursuit of the next milestone you've been trained to pursue, the next achievement you've been taught to believe will eventually make you happy.

So, how do you know who you *really* are under all that conditioning and default programming? The answer is surprisingly simple. Your true self is the 'you' that's in the driving seat in any moment of joy, when you love your life and everyone in it. It is you at your most generous, most vibrant, most brilliant best.

Have you ever been so in the flow of a conversation that your self-consciousness disappeared and, as the perfect words flowed from your mouth and around to your ears, you found yourself hearing them for the first time and wondering where they came from? Your true self is you in that zone of genius. It is how you show up when you fully connect on the inside, thinking thoughts and making choices that are in harmony with the deepest, wisest aspect of you. Your true self is your most authentic, most genuine human personality. It is the 'you' that shows up when you get out of your own way.

Connect to who you really are

Your true self is your personality in any moment where you are in alignment with your deep, wise self. This 'soul-level' self is who you are at your core. It is the keeper of your dreams and desires for yourself and for the world. It knows your strengths and your untapped talents. It knows your fundamental preferences. It knows what helps you and what hinders you in bringing *who you really are* to your work and your relationships. This deep, wise aspect of you may be outside your conscious awareness much of the time, but it knows your true power, your potential to contribute to this world in ways you have yet to even imagine. It knows the unique conditions under which you are most likely to thrive. It knows how hard you try, and appreciates you for your efforts regardless of the outcome, always nudging you towards self-appreciation, self-compassion and self-care. The real you knows that you are doing your best in every given moment, even in those moments when you temporarily give up and rage against the world or sob quietly in a corner. It is the most expansive and visionary aspect of your being – the part of you that never loses perspective, that knows in every moment that learning from setbacks is also progress. It is the aspect of your consciousness that never wavers in its love and appreciation for you, for everyone around you and for this journey we call 'life'.

It doesn't matter what you call this deep, wise, unconditionally loving core self. Depending on your world view – humanistic, scientific, religious, spiritual, etc. – you may think of it as your deep self, your quantum consciousness, your inner genius, your higher self or your soul. There is no need to debate the relative merits of one such world view over another. To do so would distract us from our purpose of setting you up to live your best life. Likewise, there is no merit in debating what to call this authentic core self – who you really are underneath that lifetime of conditioning. It only matters that you recognise that this deeply wise, loving and endlessly inspired aspect of you exists, and that you are so much more magnificent than you often know yourself to be.

For simplicity, from now on I'll be referring to the deepest and truest, core aspect of you as 'the real you' or 'who you really are'. I may occasionally use the word 'soul'. But I encourage you to map that across to whatever label – deep self, quantum consciousness, inner genius, higher self, etc. – feels best to you and aligns most fully with your own world view. All that is needed to fully benefit from the rest of this book is to understand that no matter who or what you think you are, you are always – and in all ways – more.

Cultivating a connection between 'you' as a conscious thinking personality and your deep, wise, soul-level self is the single most powerful investment you will ever make. Doing so opens up a channel of communication within you, giving you access to guidance, solutions, courage, energy and inspiration – everything you need to drive for your dreams and love the journey. We'll look at how to tune yourself to this guidance in more detail in Chapter 10, so you can harness the full power of this connection as your inner *satnav for life*. For now, let's continue to explore how you can more fully recognise your true self – your most authentic personality – so that you can reclaim this journey as your own.

Put your true self in the driving seat

At this point it may sound like I am advocating for selfishness – a major breach of the official rules of the road. So, let me be straight: in a way, I am. Not 'selfishness' in the harsh, ego-driven, winner-takes-all sense, but in the sense of listening to yourself, tuning into *what matters most* to you, and then making that your priority.

You cannot create a life you truly love if you are constantly prioritising the needs and expectations of others over your own genuine needs.

If you unwittingly sacrifice authentic self-esteem for the esteem of others whose approval depends on you continuously meeting their needs at the expense of your own, that's not service. That's martyrdom.

Now you may feel some hesitation – perhaps even a visceral fear – when you consider doing something other than what is expected of you. The early programming that led you to seek the approval, and heed the criticism, of those who did their best to raise and educate you is still running on the inside.

There is a part of you that remembers being dependent upon those authority figures for your very survival, and you carry their voices with you.

As a result, you are navigating each moment with a car full of back seat drivers telling you the next move you *must* make from here if you want to survive long enough to reach the happiness horizon where you can hopefully, eventually, finally, truly thrive.

Being *driven* in this way would be challenging enough if your back seat drivers were all in agreement, but often they argue among themselves. Each voice in your head represents a different aspect of your lifelong programming, a different subset of the rules of the road. Ever thought of sharing your work in a more visible way, only to find the part of you that believes you need to stand out gets shouted down by the part of you that believes you need to fit in? This internal conflict, this clash of programming, can be intensely stressful and at times even debilitating. It's not easy to move forward when you're not sure which way to turn. If you do press ahead, it can be exhausting, or at least not as much fun as it would be if the whole of you was pulling in the same direction. The default response to such internal conflict is to stick with what you know, to stay on the track you're already on, whether or not it's authentically yours.

And if a lifetime of conditioning wasn't enough, remember that your inner protector is also there, operating through primitive wiring that defaults to the perceived safety of fitting in. This ancient part of you has a primal fear of rejection. Historically, this made a lot of sense. For your early human ancestors, basic physical survival was a group effort, and rejection – being ousted by the tribe – was almost certainly a death sentence.

Is it any wonder then that you may sometimes feel utterly compelled to please your boss or your client by doing whatever it takes to get a project over the line, even when you know you are *harming yourself* in the process? In such moments it may feel as though somehow your life depends on getting the job done, as though the word 'deadline' is literally true! But if you act on this ancient programming without awareness and discernment, unquestioningly meeting the demands and expectations of the authority figures in your life – your boss, your clients, your partner, your parents and anyone else to whom you've unconsciously handed over your personal power – your life is not your own. You may meet your short-term needs for recognition, praise and approval – and the temporary sense of safety they bring – but you do so at the expense of your authentic need for joy, wellbeing and meaning.

Continually seeking the esteem of others can cost you your self-esteem. 'Fitting in' can stop you finding where you truly *belong*.

Grow as you go

Such primal imperatives combined with decades of conditioning can mean that turning inwards – looking to *yourself* for guidance and answers – may feel risky or even downright dangerous at first. But without it, there can be no true authenticity. Yes, there may be work to do to rebuild full confidence in yourself. You may need to learn to distinguish between your own deep wisdom and old conditioned programming about who you should *ideally* be. You may need to learn to recognise and honour your own impulses, instincts and intuitions. You may need to learn to trust that, whatever happens, you'll handle it. That learning and growth takes time, but can also be part of the fun.

There is joy to be found in acting on a loving impulse and being surprised and delighted by where it leads. There is an incomparable thrill in doing things you weren't absolutely sure you could do. Loving the journey truly begins when you put your true self in the driving seat and become the *sole authority* in your life.

Over time, you become more discerning about what you will accept and embrace and what you will not. Honouring such authentic boundaries doesn't make you more rigid or limit your freedom or flexibility. It simply makes you less malleable to the whims, demands and expectations of others. Authentic boundaries help you stay focused on what matters most.

In reclaiming this journey as your own, you will connect more fully to your deep, wise self and your own dreams and desires. As you do, you'll trigger a series of astounding discoveries about who you really are and the work you will most love to do. What's more I guarantee that *your most authentic work will be anything but selfish*. It will, without doubt, be focused on making a contribution beyond yourself – a contribution to your business, your community or the world at large.

How is it that I can give you such a bold guarantee with such confidence? The answer is simply this: it is in your true nature to be generous, to want to make a difference beyond yourself.

A life you love is built one loving impulse at a time. Kindness and generosity are love in action. Your dream destination will be a goal with soul.

Authenticity – putting your truest, most genuine, soul-guided self in the driving seat – is the key to effortless, enjoyable and sustainable success. So, if you want to thrive as you drive, it's time to embark on an astonishing journey of self-discovery. It's time to find your unique zone of genius.

7. Find Your Zone of Genius

If you are always trying to be normal,
you will never know how amazing you can be.

– Maya Angelou
American poet, memoirist and civil rights activist

Catch yourself being brilliant!

Are you ready to get to know who you really are? Are you curious to discover the innate talents and authentic strengths that you are uniquely gifted to cultivate and express? In short, are you willing to catch yourself being brilliant?

You did not arrive in this world as a blank slate, waiting to be written upon by your parents, your community and the world at large. You were born with a predisposition towards brilliance in certain areas – birthday gifts such as hand–eye coordination, a gift for music, a natural talent for connection and empathy, a way with words or an affinity for numbers. And, with guidance, experience and dedicated practice, you have cultivated some of these innate talents into fully deployable strengths. As we've already explored, the personality that you think of as 'you' is a product of both nature and nurture.

So, what is your true nature?

What is the natural sweet spot within everything you can do well – your authentic zone of genius – that flows directly from your unique combination of qualities, innate talents, authentic strengths, guiding values, experience and knowledge?

Answering this hugely important question requires that you slow down. It's an opportunity to tap into your 'still power' – reflection, curiosity, openness – because your wisest, most insightful answers cannot be forced: they can only be allowed. True self-discovery is not working things out: it's making space for your most authentic answers to be revealed.

With this in mind, I recommend approaching this exploration in two stages. The first is divergent – going broad and deep to generate as much information about yourself as possible. The second stage is convergent – homing in on the subset of qualities, strengths and skills which are most aligned with who you really are, and which you feel most inspired to cultivate and contribute to as you move forward: your authentic zone of genius.

As you explore and reflect using the power questions that follow, patterns and themes will begin to emerge. There is power in writing your answers down instead of just thinking them through, so don't be tempted to skip over this step. Take up your travel log and *capture your thoughts and ideas as you go*. Keep going or, if you prefer, come back and add to your notes several times. It's often the ideas that emerge later, once the surface-level thoughts have been captured, that are the most profoundly authentic and inspiring.

Begin by listing out everything you are good at. Take stock in both personal and professional arenas. For broad areas, such as communication or problem-solving, stay with the question longer and note every detail of what contributes to your effectiveness in that area. Ask yourself, 'What *specifically* am I good at that contributes to my success with________.'

Nobody is going to see this list but you, so soothe your inner protector's challenges and protestations and write down *everything* that comes to mind. Make the list as long as possible.

Now your journey of self-discovery is under way! You're ready for the second stage. Identifying your natural strengths and innate talents – your zone of genius – provides a key piece of the puzzle of who you really are. It points you towards your areas of greatest potential contribution.

Working in your zone of genius is also relatively effortless and enjoyable, underpinning your potential for *sustainable success*, shifting the emphasis from relying on strengths that drain you as you use them to those *authentic* strengths that actually energise you as you work.

There's just one small catch. Our innate talents and predispositions are so natural, so much a part of who we are, that they tend to be outside our conscious awareness. We often don't know *how* we do what we do so well – we just do it. And that means that the long list you just came up with is probably nowhere near as long as it could and should be. Most of us are most aware of those skills and strengths that took blood, sweat and tears to develop. But look beyond those hard-won abilities to the skills, strengths and talents that make a difference for others, but which come *easily and naturally* for you.

Clues from your journey so far

Revisit the list you began above, and broaden it further by considering the following questions:

- ✦ When do people come to you and ask for help? Be it colleagues, friends or extended family, what struggles do others bring to you? Are there any patterns to what these have in common? And what skills, strengths and personal qualities do these requests reflect?
- ✦ When do people thank you profusely for a contribution that, for you, was a no-brainer? It's easy to dismiss such feedback as over the top, since for you it's not rocket science. But remember that ease and flow are indicators of authenticity.

- ✦ When do you feel surprised, perplexed or frustrated by others' inability to 'keep up'? Instead of seeing these moments as inadequacies in others (as you were trained to), recognise these moments as indicators of your own natural abilities.
- ✦ What, if anything, did you get into trouble for as a child? And what qualities, characteristics and talents does this suggest? For example, if you got into trouble for talking in class, this might point to a gift for communication, playfulness, social intelligence, etc.
- ✦ What do you read/consume for pleasure? When you choose books, podcasts, talks and other resources, where does your natural curiosity take you?
- ✦ When do you feel most fully alive? What are you doing? And what qualities, passions, strengths and skills are you bringing to those activities and experiences?

The more you reflect on these questions, the more you will discover about *who you really are*, and what you bring when you're at your brilliant best. And even though we are just beginning our exploration, there's no need to wait.

You can begin right now to consider how you might connect more consistently to your zone of genius, allowing your work to become an outlet for authentic self-expression and contribution.

This is the way of being and doing that underpins everything that you love to experience and create. And when you bring who you really are to the moment, everybody wins.

As your list grows, you will begin to spot patterns, recurring themes that emerge no matter what question you explore or angle you adopt. These themes are underpinned by your most innate talents and preferences. This might be your preference for focusing on tasks or connecting with people; making high-level strategic connections or paying exquisite attention to detail; being guided by cool logic or heartfelt values; developing complex concepts or finding simple, practical solutions; thinking or doing; designing or delivering; proactively planning or spontaneously responding. These themes – these authentic preferences – are the basis on which you can reshape and re-energise your current role, as well as the enablers of your most enjoyable, rewarding and sustainable future success.

Shortcuts to insight

So how can you get even clearer on who you are and what you're uniquely gifted to bring? The good news is there are shortcuts. They come in the form of profiling tools which, if used intelligently, can give you an extraordinarily well-rounded view of both your existing strengths and your untapped potential.

There is a wide range of such profiling tools available, each designed with a specific focus in mind. When seeking to discover your innate zone of genius, the tools I have found most helpful – both personally and when working with my clients – are those that look much deeper than surface-level skills and knowledge. These – see the Resources at the end of the book for links – include:

- Broad assessments of your character and personality preferences, such as Myers-Briggs, Sparketype and DiSC
- Assessments of character strengths as revealed by the VIA Strengths Inventory
- Profiling tools that focus on core capabilities and behavioural strengths, as assessed by the Clifton-Strengths (Gallup) and Strengths Profile (Cappfinity).

Beyond these are a plethora of specific profiling tools to support you in taking stock of your work-related skills and competencies – some generic, others specific to the profession, industry or sector you're in.

Some profiling tools can only be accessed by engaging with a qualified practitioner who can skilfully guide you through the information that results, and help you make the most of the insights the profile offers. Others are easily accessible online, either free or for a small fee. Either way, the key to making the most of these shortcuts to self-discovery is in using them appropriately and with discernment.

Begin by choosing and completing just one of the above profiling tools. Ensure you are as relaxed as possible and in a good space, mentally and emotionally. Even if you are completing a work-related profile, you may find it helpful to fill in the questionnaire while relaxing at home one evening or at the weekend, or at least at the start of the working day before the world grabs you by the shoulders and starts demanding your attention. This will ensure that your answers most closely reflect who you really are, and not who you are when squeezed and stressed. This is particularly important if your current work does not feel like a good fit for you. If you respond to the questionnaire in 'work mode', you may find you profile your job description instead of yourself.

The next step is to ensure that you further personalise the information you receive by reviewing your report several times and making it your own. Profiling tools offer powerful insights but are based on models that inevitably feature generalisations. It's crucial to use your own judgement to individualise the information you receive. A quick first read through is fine, but then slow right down. Feel your way into what resonates as *true for you* and what doesn't. If you move too fast, you may take the whole thing as being true, missing important nuanced distinctions. Alternatively, you may dismiss out of hand a potentially powerful insight that doesn't seem true at first glance, but which on reflection may illuminate a blind spot, an internal barrier that might hold you back or an authentic but unrealised talent that you've not previously recognised or explored.

Print out a copy of your report and mark it up with your thoughts as you go. In addition to a standard pen for note taking, you may find it helpful to also have two others at hand: a highlighter and a thick black marker.

The highlighter pen is to highlight the phrases and insights that resonate with you most fully and deeply. If you later reread the highlights only, this makes pattern-spotting so much easier. You'll also find that these highlights put into words aspects of who you are that at some level you've always known but which you've perhaps struggled to articulate. Having a way of expressing these fundamental qualities, character traits and strengths can be invaluable in a whole host of situations, such as during interviews, performance review/career conversations and even when updating your social media profiles and CV.

The thick black marker is for striking out any lines that do *not* resonate as true for you at all, or which perhaps were once true but no longer apply. This might include common blind spots for people who share your personality preferences, but which you've previously recognised and already overcome.

Mapping your zone of genius

It can be extremely helpful to complete a number of different profiles that focus on different aspects of your zone of genius. Doing so gives a richer map of who you are and what you are gifted to bring to the world. It also makes the pattern-spotting even easier, as any core aspects of who you are will run through the various reports as recurring themes.

Profiling tools can offer invaluable insights into who you are and into your authentic zone of genius, but remember that they are only shortcuts to self-discovery. They can never fully map the richness and complexity of your inner world, and that's a good thing.

Self-discovery can be an inner journey as surprising and delightful as any adventure on the outside, and last your whole life long.

The more you discover about who you really are, the more you can enjoy evolving in the direction of the most brilliant human you have the potential to be, and the greater the meaningful impact you can have.

When you put your true self in the driving seat, you will feel called towards the work you were born for. This work could take many forms. There is no preset destiny, no 'one right answer', but rather a myriad specific forms this work might take. What they all have in common is that it feels like *nothing is missing because the real you is present.*

From this authentic place, work rarely even feels like work. You may pour a great deal of energy into what you are doing, but there is little effort involved because there is so little internal resistance to struggle against. All your energy goes into what you are creating and contributing in the moment, and everyone around you benefits. You're aligned with your dream destination, pedal to the metal and the brakes are off.

Who's in your wings?

And if you want to see the opportunity that's all around you, remember you've got wing mirrors too, and they can be even more powerful. They allow you to see what cannot be seen directly. They help you to see your surroundings more clearly – not only your scenery, but yourself. And the light bouncing off your fellow travellers can illuminate, inform and energise your authentic journey. So, check out your wing mirrors and notice who comes into view.

Who do you most admire – in your current organisation, your extended family or your community? It may be someone you worked for in the past, someone the rest of us may never know but who made an indelible impression on you at the time. It may even be someone from your childhood or teen years – a parent, a teacher, a youth leader. It could even be a figure from history, perhaps a pioneer in your field of expertise – someone you know only through their writing, speeches or another creative legacy.

Tune yourself more fully to the person you most admire, and imagine they are here with you now. What do you notice about the choices they make? What values or principles inspire and guide them? How do they behave towards others or respond in the face of a significant challenge? What abilities have they cultivated into strengths, perhaps even superpowers? What personal qualities do they embody, day in and day out? It's not necessary that you admire *everything* about them. It's OK to be selective. Notice what comes to mind and write everything down. Follow the feeling of *resonance*.

Now read back what you've written. Tap into your still power – relaxed, open and curious – and read *slowly*. Allow yourself to feel the resonance and recognise one crucially important and inspiring fact:

You were describing your own zone of genius – both your well-developed strengths and qualities, and your innate talents, your untapped potential for more. Let that sink in.

This may not be easy to accept, particularly if the person who came to mind is known and greatly admired by many. Your inner protector may send up warning flares that you're veering towards arrogance, narcissism or even a dangerous degree of complacency: 'Who do you think you are?' But recognising your own untapped potential is not arrogance, it's inspiration. It's a glimpse of the person you have the potential to become.

Still want to validate the correlation between who you admire and who you really are? Sometimes this is easier to see with the help of someone else.

Ask a friend or colleague – someone with a different personality to you, but whose good judgement you trust – who *they* most admire. Then ask them why. Do you agree with their choice? Do you feel the same degree of resonance? Or has your colleague chosen someone you wouldn't necessarily choose, but who reflects the qualities, values and untapped potential you can clearly see in them?

There is certainly no one right way to be in this world. Resonance is a clue to *your* right way. If you want to see more clearly who you are destined to become, make good use of your wing mirrors. See who you really are, reflected in the best qualities of those you most admire. Accept the invitation to get out of your own way and embrace the authentic adventure that unfolds as you show up more fully as your true self.

Growing your zone of genius

So now we see even more clearly that your most authentic adventure is not one journey but the continuous blending of two journeys: the outer journey of creation, connection and contribution and the inner journey of self-discovery, expansion and evolution. Both journeys involve exploration and lead to delightful discoveries. Both depend on cultivating high-quality relationships. Both result in growth.

Society's conditioned route map for success focuses almost exclusively on the outer journey. This leads to a race for results at almost any cost. Even learning is framed as a means to an end, with young people expected to gain qualifications whether or not they gain a valuable education, and professionals encouraged to acquire knowledge as a means of getting ahead. It says little if anything about the fun that can be found through lifelong learning, especially if you focus on cultivating your natural talents. As we've already explored, unless you're very fortunate, this hard-driving external focus leads to the *pursuit* of happiness at the expense of the *experience* of it.

The inner journey, on the other hand, energises and inspires as it unfolds. As you grow in your awareness of your unique strengths and innate talents, you begin to recognise your most authentic desires – the difference you want to make in your own life, in the lives of those around you and in the world as a whole. You recognise opportunities to bring more of who you really are to every task, enthusiastically stretching yourself to rise to the challenge, and increasingly experiencing yourself as being the right person in the right place at the right time. It is this focus on growth that allows you to experience even the most trying of circumstances as having meaning and great purpose in your own authentic adventure.

Committing with enthusiasm to your own growth and evolution – being open to learning, to developing new skills, and even to the potential to be transformed by your experience – leads to a new way of thinking about resilience. This new way does not require you to remain constantly hyper-vigilant, to brace yourself against the world or to be naturally thick skinned.

Resilient and ready for the twists and turns

Cultivating resilience – the ability to stay on track no matter what happens, and bounce back quickly and completely from adversity – is not about being more tough minded: it's a shift in mindset.

Authentic resilience is a shift from bracing yourself against life to embracing life exactly as it shows up.

The power unleashed when you make this commitment goes far beyond simply navigating life's challenges with your sanity intact. As you learn to trust in the inherent goodness of life – recognising that every experience will offer you the chance to 'win' (achieve) and/or to 'learn' (set yourself up to achieve in future) – you relax into the task, challenge or opportunity before you. This is a good thing because, as we'll explore more in later chapters, it's almost impossible to do your best thinking and problem-solving while your brain and nervous system are in fear mode. Learning to relax into the moment and cultivate a thrilling new form of focus, even when the stakes are high, is the basis of your authentic success. As Abraham Maslow, humanistic psychologist and originator of the classic hierarchy of needs, so insightfully put it, 'One can choose to go back toward safety or forward toward growth. Growth must be chosen again and again; fear must be overcome again and again.' (1966)

As you set your sights on a dream destination so inspiring and meaningful to you that it makes you lick your lips in anticipation, the chances are you'll also experience a certain amount of fear as you recognise you do not yet have everything you need for the journey. This increased self-awareness will inspire growth, and your new growth will inspire a new level of self-confidence as you make the contribution you increasingly feel you were born to make.

Building a healthy appetite for *managed risks* helps you cultivate the courage and confidence you need to live your life fully and freely.

As you move forward, build magical momentum and realise your dream, a new dream destination will be inspired within you – one which will further increase your self-awareness, inspire greater growth and authentic self-confidence and lead to an even more magnificent dream. So we can see that your authentic adventure is not merely cyclical, but creates an ongoing upwards spiral of growth and contribution, the inner and outer journeys blending in support of a great life.

So how can you know what career and life choices would be joyfully authentic for you? Under decades of conditioning, how can you know what you really want? It's time to find out.

8. It's Time for a Treasure Hunt

Whatever you can do or dream you can, begin it;
Boldness has genius, power, and magic in it.

– Johann Wolfgang von Goethe
German playwright and philosopher
(as lyrically translated by Irish poet John Anster in 1835)

So where is 'there' for you?

Do you know where you're going? Do you wake each morning with a profound sense of purpose, excited to begin your day? Can you see a golden thread of meaning running through everything on your to-do list and meetings schedule, connecting you to what matters most? In short, do you have a dream destination calling you forward, an inspiring goal with soul?

Authentic success, as we've already explored, is getting there while loving here. So where is 'there' for you? Where do you ultimately want to arrive? And what do you most want to create, contribute and experience along the way – the magical milestones that let you know you're on track? What is your dream destination?

If you don't yet know, that's OK. Many of my clients have gone on to create profoundly joyful and meaningful careers and lives without ever feeling the need to define a long-term future goal. Instead, they've committed to putting their unique zone of genius to work and to stretch themselves to grow their zone of genius over time. But if you are curious to discover a truly authentic vision for your future, then this chapter will offer you a treasure trail of clues.

Are you ready to look beyond the years of fear-based conditioning warning you to 'be realistic', to stick rigidly to well-worn routes to professional success, or even to sacrifice yourself at the altar of Other People's Dreams. If so, it's time to listen in on what your inner adventurer has been trying to tell you, perhaps for a very long time.

Let's acknowledge that that's going to rouse your inner protector – your internalised voice of safety. Even now, a few paragraphs in, your inner protector may be kicking in with objections, reminding you to be modest in your ambitions, to stick with what you know, to set only small goals, if any at all. Why court potential disappointment, humiliation, rejection by reaching for something big? Can you hear the screech as your emergency brake slams on?

If so, just remember that such fear-based thinking is well intentioned but fundamentally flawed. It's the thinking that, as Henry David Thoreau so poignantly acknowledged in *Walden*, leaves many leading 'lives of quiet desperation'. You cannot create and experience your best life – your most authentic, joyful and high-contributing life – by thinking 'realistically'. Your inner protector asks for near certainty upfront before making any kind of courageous move, and certainty is something our complex and ever-changing world can rarely if ever provide. Even more importantly, thinking 'realistically' is overly cautious in the extreme.

Focusing on what seems to be reasonably achievable from where you are now fails to factor in the personal growth, guiding mentors and other resources you'll rendezvous with as your journey unfolds.

It also fails to allow for the magical momentum achievable when you're inspired towards a worthy and personally meaningful goal. It fails to account for the energising effects of switching from willpower to thrill power.

Dreaming big – allowing yourself to feel your way into your most magnificent vision for yourself and the world – transforms change and uncertainty from a threat to an ally. When nothing is certain, anything is possible. And a focus on possibility allows you to set out for your authentic dream destination without the need to know the details of exactly *how* you'll get there. Embracing uncertainty creates space for serendipity, space for the opportunities and assistance you could not have imagined in advance. A focus on your dream destination, combined with real-time decision-making, sets you up to experience thrill power to the max.

So, reassure your inner protector that this exploration is just an *inner* adventure for now. We're about to embark on an *internal* hunt for treasure, a search for insights about who you really are and what you really want to create and contribute. The pages that follow offer you the opportunity to consider fresh possibilities, a chance to listen to what your inner adventurer has to say. Safety is not being cast aside, or caution thrown to the wind. As you'll soon discover, the true magic of life happens as your inner protector and inner adventurer work together to realise your dreams.

Your dream destination is calling

Your dream destination is a point of focus on the far horizon. It is the set of extraordinary circumstances with which you'd most love to rendezvous. It's not just what you'll *have* when you get there – the abundance of ideas, rich relationships and resources galore – though creating all of that can certainly be part of the fun. Your authentic dream destination also represents the difference you most want to make in the world, the goal with soul that puts you firmly in touch with your own untapped potential.

Your dream destination
calls you forward and
calls forward the best in you.

Your dream destination is unique to you. It is the meeting place of who you really are and what the world really needs. It flows directly from your zone of genius, and is the inspiration behind your most meaningful and joyful contribution. In any moment when you are meeting a genuine need in the world, your actions can feel meaningful. But it's only when that genuine need aligns with who you really are that you'll truly feel like the right person in the right place at the right time. Even in the midst of harsh challenges, meeting genuine needs and growing yourself in the process can feel like a significant stage of your authentic adventure. Focusing in the direction of what you want, riding the momentum you've created and bringing your whole self to the moment. This is the stuff of life!

So how can you discover your dream destination? How can you discern what's truly yours and not merely a conditioned 'ideal' based on society's, or the corporate world's, one-size-fits-all route map? How can you ensure you're headed towards your own dream destination and not someone else's?

The good news is that, every day of your life, you've been offered a continuous stream of clues. The real you has been guiding you in every moment towards what is for you, and away from what is not. Now is the time to leverage all your experience to date, from the most painful to the most pleasurable, and discover your most authentic way forward from here.

The time has come for you to embark on a most exciting treasure hunt. It's time to scavenge for even more clues as to who you really are, so that you can more clearly envision what a truly 'you-shaped' life could look like.

Let the treasure hunt begin

As a driver, you want to make swift progress, safely and sustainably, and enjoy the ride. To support you in these aims you have three key resources at your disposal:

- your *windscreen*, showing you the road ahead and allowing you to scan the far horizon
- your *rear-view mirror*, showing you how far you've come, and helping you predict what's behind you now but might soon be alongside or ahead
- your *wing mirrors and windows*, showing you who and what is alongside you here and now.

As a driver on this journey of life, the same three perspectives are available to you. Each can offer an abundance of data, rich insights and fuel for your imagination.

In the previous chapter, you checked your wing mirrors. You noticed the drivers around you, and reflected on who feels closest, who resonates with you most fully. As you considered who you most admire, and what specifically it is about them that you deeply appreciate, your wing mirrors offered you glimpses of your own potential for greatness. Now let's make the most of your other two perspectives.

First you'll scan the horizon. As you clear your windscreen and look ahead as far as the eye can see, you'll notice what's there for you. What future have you already been imagining? What do you love about the trajectory you're already on, and what feels bland or even fills you with dread? What fleeting glimpses can you catch of something extraordinary on the horizon when you feel your way into a goal with soul?

Next you'll check your rear-view mirror. When you reflect on your journey to date, can you see how far you've come? What moments so far do you most deeply treasure, those peak experiences seared into your memory as the best of life? What experiences at work and in life have been most unwanted, and what can they tell you about what you truly wish to experience from here? What can your journey so far tell you about your criteria for your most authentic and satisfying onward journey?

Once you gather your treasure trove of insights, you'll have the chance to envision your authentic dream destination. Beyond your current skills and experience, beyond any perceived lack of resources – time, money, know-how, contacts, mentors – you'll see it, calling you forward and calling forward the best in you.

Scan your horizon

To begin, let's look at where you're currently headed. Let's scan the shimmering horizon to see what's already there. You're on your way to somewhere, whether deliberately or by default. So, let's spritz the windscreen, and take a clear, long-range view.

As you look out onto the far horizon, what do you see? If you continue on your current trajectory, where might you be a year from now? Three years from now? Five years? When you imagine your future from here, do you like what you see – not only what you've accomplished and accumulated, but the status of your health, relationships and general enthusiasm for life? Or does a clear windscreen – a willingness to see *all* of what's on the horizon, without denying the unwanted aspects – suggest a realignment is required?

And what if you look even further ahead? Ten years from now? Twenty years or more from now? The choices you make here and now create the future you will live. Based on your current trajectory, are you on course to love the life you've created when you get there?

The longer the time frame, the greater the uncertainty in any prediction, but also the greater the untapped possibility. A small change of direction now can take you to a very different destination in the future.

Look out once again to the far horizon. If you scan for what's new and different, what glimpses of brilliance catch your eye? Even if those gleaming new possibilities are not yet clear, wobbling in the heat haze of high summer, notice what draws your attention and triggers a rush of thrill power here and now. Catch the flashes of possibility that offer themselves up as you let go of your doubt and resistance and allow yourself to dream big.

What would you pursue if success was guaranteed? More authentically still, what would be worth the attempt even if you came up short in some way – worthwhile for the growth, the learning and the contribution that even a partial success could bring?

As you write, allow a stream of consciousness to flow to you and through you, uncensored and uncontrived. Forget punctuation and 'proper English'. Let your pen move at pace. Be curious about what will be revealed if you drop your awareness from up in your head down into your body. When you shift out of your intellect, and instead *feel* your way forward, what do you notice? Trust what you're shown – even if it doesn't seem to make sense at first – and stay curious. What vision comes into focus when you allow yourself to imagine your most inspired life? Take fear out of the equation just long enough to fully consider what your dream destination could look like. Quieten your inner protector just long enough to notice what your inner adventurer wants you to see.

Now, if you're still imagining your dream destination from a distance, looking ahead from here and now, notice what happens when you shift your perspective. Zoom into that vision on your far horizon. Be *there* now. Allow the scene to unfold in its own time, unguided by you. Be patient and curious, and wait to be shown, as you consider the following questions:

1. If a miracle happened and you were suddenly living the life of your dreams, where do you see yourself? Notice the small details that may surprise you, such as how you are dressed, what you're eating or the climate of where you now live. What do these small, perhaps unexpected, details tell you about what matters most?
2. On an ideal day, or in an ideal week, how are you spending your time? What work are you doing that doesn't feel like work most of the time? What problems are you solving, and what

opportunities are you creating? Who is there with you – your convoy of colleagues, friends and loved ones – exploring, achieving and celebrating together?

3. And how are you feeling as your mental movie unfolds? What is the essence of your emotional experience, the basis of your quality of life? Are you joyful, playful, light hearted? Are you curious, stimulated, engaged? Are you connected, uplifted, in love? Are you contented, peaceful, deeply satisfied? Are you fulfilled yet enthusiastic, inspired and ready for more? Notice the emotional landscape of your dream destination. How are you living – fully, freely, vibrantly alive – when you arrive?

Trust what you are shown. Don't dismiss what you see as 'too big', unrealistic, unachievable. Stay curious. What you envision may be intended literally as a new and different path, or it may be a metaphor or symbol intended to inspire your most joyful journey on the path you're already on. Let your inner adventurer have their say.

And if your answers are not immediately clear, that's fine too. Just keep coming back to the questions. Your vision will soon come into sharp relief, and you'll be able to draw even greater energy and inspiration from the details and contours of your dream destination.

Check your rear-view mirror

Now let's make good use of your rear-view mirror. It's time to see what dreams from your past might hold clues for your future. And it's a very good time to reflect on your past experiences of both joy and disappointment, to look at how far you've come, and to once again see what themes and patterns emerge that might help show you the way.

As a child, what did you want to be when you grew up? Your earliest dreams may have been inspired by your favourite movies and most cherished toys – doctor, baker, maybe even a dinosaur wrangler! Maybe you left those early dreams behind fairly readily, as your awareness of the genuine possibilities expanded. And yet, the essence of your favoured option may offer insights today, *if* you notice the idea still delivers a frisson of excitement and inspiration. The doctor's ability to relieve suffering and restore wellness. The baker's ability to nourish and bring delight. Even the dinosaur-wrangler's skill, responsiveness and sense of adventure! Long-forgotten childhood dreams, whether rooted in reality or fantasy, can offer insights into who you really are and the work you were born to do.

And what of the dreams that came later, the ideas and inspirations you explored and perhaps even pursued for a while? Is it possible that, when you dismissed the idea, you let go of something that's deeply authentic to you? For example, towards the end of my school career I briefly considered going into teaching. However, my only reference point for 'teacher' at that time was my own experience of the school system. The vision this inspired was of the joy of facilitating learning in the interested few, hugely outweighed by the frustrations of being stuck in with a room full of teenagers, most of whom didn't want to be there. My limited view of what was possible within the school system – let alone my complete lack of awareness of the possibilities to 'teach' in business and beyond – meant I dismissed the idea of teaching and took another route. It was only during my 'early midlife crisis', reflecting on my career to date at age 29, that I realised I was happiest and most deeply satisfied when facilitating learning in others, helping to unleash their untapped and authentic potential. I recognised a fundamental truth: I was, at some level, born to teach.

Your dreams of the past, if ever you had them, can be a powerful starting point for your reflections, helping you to tune to your most inspired life. But what if, like many of my coaching clients, you've never really known what you wanted? What if you simply followed the guidance of the parents, teachers and youth leaders that got you started, and then made go-with-the-flow choices from there? No problem! You don't have to look back quite so far to find powerful insights, and inspire your most purposeful and enjoyable journey from here.

What childhood dreams did you hold for a while and then release, which are worth revisiting now from your broader adult perspective? If you dust off the cobwebs and look again, what treasures can you find in your dreams of the past? What still resonates today? And what new possibilities for the future do these insights suggest?

Life offers you clues, all day every day, as to who you really are and who you are not.

When have you most enjoyed the journey?

The real you – your soul-level self – has been guiding and nudging you all day every day. But as you were trained to look outside yourself for answers, the chances are you haven't yet fully capitalised on the guidance you've been given. So let's look at some of your most brilliant experiences to date – the moments when you felt most vibrantly alive – so you can reflect on what they have in common. By fully considering what was true for you in a peak experience or favourite role, and then another and another, you can begin to see the clear themes that emerge. These themes are *your criteria for authentic happiness and job satisfaction*, and you can rediscover or recreate these conditions through the choices you make from here.

For many of us, meaningful work is at the heart of a meaningful and satisfying life. It's the chance to rise each morning with a sense of purpose, a focal point for discovery, creativity or contribution, the chance to fire up your thrill power and make a living by making a difference. With your true self in the driving seat, work rarely feels like work. So grab your travel journal again, and let's check your rear-view mirror and see what's there from the perspective you have today.

Think of a time in your career when you were particularly happy and satisfied. It doesn't have to be your whole role at the time. It may instead have been a particular aspect of your work, perhaps something that was not even part of your official job description. It may even have been just one really great day. What comes to mind when you trawl your memory for a highlight of your career so far? Fully immerse yourself in your memories of that experience. Write down anything and everything that comes to mind about what was true for you at that time. Highlight only what you appreciated most and, for now, park anything that 'could've been better'.

- What was the nature of the work itself?
- What was the purpose that inspired the work?
- How did you approach the tasks and challenges your work presented?
- What skills, strengths and interests did your work draw upon?
- Where did you work, and what did you appreciate most about that environment?
- Who were you working with, and how would you characterise your relationships with your colleagues, your boss, your senior leadership team, your clients?
- What were the most positive aspects of how you were managed, mentored or led?
- What did you learn, and how did your work support your growth and more recent contributions?

Once you've explored the first career highlight that came to mind, begin again with a second. When or where *else* were you particularly happy and satisfied? Again, fully consider what was true for you at the time, in terms of the nature of the work, your relationships, the way you were managed, and beyond. And from there, can you find and consider a third example? Perhaps even a fourth?

As you explore each career highlight in turn, you'll see that patterns and themes begin to emerge, patterns that combine to describe your sweet spot for job satisfaction. Perhaps you're at your happiest in the buzz of collaborating closely with others or when working independently and without interruption. Perhaps you've relished working for bosses who gave you clear instruction and ongoing guidance or for hands-off bosses who clearly stated the desired result and left the 'how' entirely up to you. Perhaps you've most enjoyed designing and refining systems and processes or creating physical products. Perhaps you've been at your happiest unleashing the untapped potential of a gap in the market or of the people around you. Reread what you've written and look for the themes that run through each of your peak experiences. There are no rights and wrongs, just right and wrong *for you*, your personal criteria for job satisfaction.

The above exercise is a wonderful way to tap into your genuine preferences. These broad insights alone can be invaluable in navigating future career crossroads, and can help you keep your true self in the driving seat more easily and more of the time. If you want to go deeper, there is a second stage that can help you get even clearer and far more specific about what's *uniquely* true for you.

The hidden treasures of challenging terrain

Over the years I've noticed that my clients are far more acutely aware of what matters most to them when discussing experiences when their needs were *not* met, when they were deeply unhappy or dissatisfied at work. This may seem strange at first, but is to be expected when you remember the way your brain and nervous system respond when triggered into stress. When you're in any kind of pain – including emotional distress – your inner protector focuses intensely on your environment, with a view to spotting a potential way out. And that means these stressful, painful moments are also packed with insight if you take just a few minutes to reflect. By turning those unwanted conditions around to their natural opposite, you put yourself even more richly in touch with what you truly want in your career from here.

Bring to mind a low point in your career, one where you were particularly *unhappy and dissatisfied*. In your travel log, begin a second list, or stream of consciousness, and notice what was true for you at that difficult time. Review the questions above again, to fully consider the nature of the work, your environment, your relationships. What contributed to your difficulty, discomfort or distress? Having thoroughly explored one example, identify a second and then a third.

Now take each 'pain point', each factor that

contributed to your distress, and ask yourself, 'What is the opposite of this for me?' For example, if you wrote how painful it was being micromanaged, ask yourself, 'What is the opposite of that for me?' The first 'opposite' might come to mind quite readily – for example, being given space. Then you might notice that there is more than one way of turning around being micromanaged to its natural opposite for you, such as having autonomy or being trusted. At the other end of the spectrum, you may have written about being left floundering by your boss, unsure of what was needed or expected. In that case the opposites might include clear guidance, clear metrics, constructive feedback, support, encouragement, and so on. For each pain point you've identified, stay for a while longer, look for new opposites, and notice what else is there. Remember there are no absolute rights and wrongs here; just invaluable insights about what's right for you and wrong for you.

As you review this second list of criteria for job satisfaction, you will see once again that themes emerge. Some of these will already appear on the first list you wrote, but others will be new. Add them in now for an expanded view of the conditions that have helped you thrive in the past, and which underpin your most authentic, high-contributing and sustainable success from here.

The essence of your dream is available now

I hope that, as you review this list, you're enjoying a delicious 'Aha!' moment, seeing clearly for perhaps the first time why your current role and the career path you're already on are such a good fit. If so, having conscious awareness of this sweet spot will help you increase your job satisfaction, and perhaps even tweak the emphasis of your role and any associated objectives to enhance the fit still further.

But perhaps you look at that list and think, 'Uh-oh... I'm badly off course. So few of these needs are being met right now.' And if that's the case, that's great information too. Let this be your moment of radical self-honesty. Celebrate the fact that you now understand more clearly than ever why your current role is such a poor fit. You now have your criteria for job satisfaction, which can be factored into the role rescope, job hunt or business launch that will take you forward. Instead of simply escaping your current role, with all the attendant risks of recreating your unhappiness elsewhere, you can plan for success. You can focus on building in happiness and maximising your contribution as you actively shape your career from here.

When you are intentional about putting your true self in the driving seat and bringing your authentic zone of genius to your work, everyone wins. So, look how far you've come, see what you've created and who you've already become.

You do not have to wait until you are fully locked on to your long-term goal with soul. You are already surrounded by a never-ending stream of opportunities to make a difference, while significantly increasing your job satisfaction. Yes, your dream destination is calling you, but the opportunity to align more with your zone of genius is available to you here and now. Let's explore more how you can thrive as you drive right here, right now.

Pull your attention back from that far horizon, and take in the scenery right where you are. Glance out of the windows from side to side and see what's already within easy reach. Fully consider where, when and how you can put your zone of genius to work right here, right now. What could you do more of? What activities could you refocus, delegate or ditch altogether? How could you reshape your role so it is the best possible fit for you, and what would be the benefits of this to your boss, your team and your organisation? How could you add even more value by creating the conditions that allow you to do your best, most brilliant, most enjoyable work?

Yes, your journey will move you in the direction of your dream destination. But the essence of that destination – the joy of being your true self and making your most authentic contribution – is available to you here and now.

9. Discover Your Dream Destination

Set a goal so big that you can't achieve it until you grow into the person who can.

– Anonymous

Dream big!

You've scanned the far horizon for gleaming possibilities. You've checked your rear-view mirror for the clues life has offered you so far. And you've taken in the scenery around you, acknowledging the aspects of your work and life that already match your dream destination. Now the time has come for you to pull together everything you've found on your treasure hunt so far. It's time to home in on your most authentic dream destination – the most extraordinary, growth-promoting and high-contributing vision of your future.

Now it's important to say at this point that 'dreaming big' does not necessarily involve a dream that would be big in other people's eyes. It's a dream that feels purposeful and deeply meaningful, something big and important to *you*. And you know how it feels when you're up to something big. So let yourself follow that feeling towards something authentic and extraordinary to you, a goal worthy of your time, energy and attention. A destination that will call you forward and call forward the best in you.

At this point there are two potential traps which could get in the way of you identifying your most authentic dream destination. The first is in visualising your *idealised* or *conditioned* destination rather than envisioning your most *authentic* dream. If a great deal has always been expected of you – as a child, as a student, a bright recruit – then the destination you're locked on to may be someone else's big dream and not your own. This is the trap of continuing to pursue what you were taught would bring success and happiness without fully considering the work and life that fits who you really are at your core. Conversely, if you were *not* well-supported as a child, or little has been expected of you since, then your dream may be too *small for you* – a reflection of others' low expectations, rather than an authentic and inspiring choice based on the truth of who you are.

The second trap is having your inner protector in the driving seat as you attempt to set your course. This can lead to paralysis by analysis. Your inner protector will want far more detail about *how* any dream might be achieved than is likely to be available in the beginning, and that uncertainty can cause you to scale back your aspirations. It's well intentioned, but it's a mistake. It can rob you of the joy of the journey now, and create the risk of later regret.

Small dreams – or, worse still, an unwillingness to dream at all – leave you languishing in a life that is less than you want or deserve. Your inner protector may be trying to shield you from the risk of disappointment. But if you don't dare to dream, your disappointment is almost guaranteed.

In the pages that follow, you'll discover four simple yet powerful approaches that can help you navigate your way around the above traps with relative ease. This first approach helps you access your still power, remembering that your most authentic and transformational ideas cannot come from your intellect alone and connecting more fully to the wisdom held in your body. Try it now.

Place your hand across your heart. Apply a gentle pressure. Notice what happens to the rate of your breathing, and to the location of its rise and fall (chest, ribs, belly). And notice any subtle shifts in how you feel.

Now, take up your travel log. With your hand still in place, begin to review all the notes you've written so far as you've explored who you really are, your authentic zone of genius, and the glimpses of your untapped potential reflected in those you most admire. Notice what else you are ready to add.

Relish the suspense

As you settle into your still power, connecting your powerful intellect with the wisdom of your heart and your gut, remember this crucial point:

Anything can be visualised, but your authentic path must be *envisioned.*

Visualisation is using your imagination purposefully. If I invite you to visualise the Pyramids of Egypt, you can probably do it. In fact, you almost certainly just did. But envisioning is a different experience. Envisioning is relaxing back and waiting for something to be revealed, waiting to be shown.

Here's a fun approach that will help you access the open and curious state that is optimal for envisioning.

Imagine visiting your favourite cinema and taking a comfortable seat. You're about to be shown a wonderful movie, one you've been wanting to see for a long time. You don't know the specifics of what you'll see on the screen – and the suspense is part of the fun. But you do know this movie features all your favourite actors, and it's going to be amazing! Sit comfortably – metaphorical popcorn in hand, relaxed and curious, yet alive with anticipation – and *wait to be shown*. What can you see and hear, and how do you feel, as you immerse yourself with curiosity in the mental movie of life at your dream destination?

Now, any great movie is even better when shared with a real-life friend. Sometimes we miss important insights when we only reflect alone, but the chance to talk things through with someone else can add depth and breadth to our perception.

Who do you know, *like and trust* who would enjoy exploring this with you – and perhaps their own dream destination too? This could be a friend or member of your extended family, or a professional friend, teacher or mentor. Who is close enough to you to care, but far enough away to be a little more objective? Who could help challenge your assumptions about what's possible, and inspire you towards an even bolder vision for yourself and your life? In short, who do you know who has no vested interest in the status quo, and can help you to dream big?

Ask them for help or invite them to buddy up and help them too. Don't overthink it. Ask them, call them, message them now!

Choose your horizon

As you await their response, begin envisioning your authentic dream destination. Start by noticing the time frame you feel excited to explore. For most of my clients this tends to be their dream destination at around three to five years from now, though it can be much longer. Some are excited to explore their *ultimate* dream – what they'd love to create, contribute and experience in their career or this lifetime. Of course, you can do both. Just notice what feels like the most natural and inspiring horizon to explore as a starting point.

And ask yourself the question, 'What's possible for *someone like me*?' Notice the question is not, 'What's possible for me?' The chances are your limiting assumptions, your barriers of belief, will sneak in swiftly if you attempt to brainstorm for yourself. But if you focus on the question 'What's possible for *someone like* me?', you open up the field of possibilities.

Imagine you are brainstorming with, and on behalf of, a close friend or loved one. Imagine this is someone you admire and appreciate – someone with your talents, your strengths, your passions, your experience, your desire to make a difference and your commitment to a lifetime of joyful personal growth and expansion. What would you suggest was possible for *them*?

Now remember, 'possible' doesn't mean 'definitely achievable'. You do not need to have any of the 'how' all figured out yet. You're at the ideas stage and, as Nobel Prize-winning physicist Linus Pauling is believed to have said, 'The best way to get a good idea is to get lots of ideas.' So, for now, just suspend judgement. Your inner protector will have an important role to play soon, helping you sift and sort through the options, and helping you make incredible progress intelligently, safely and sustainably. But now is *not* the time for evaluation. Now is the time to tune even more fully to your inner adventurer and let them have their say.

The more often you visit your dream destination in your mind – with an attitude of openness and curiosity – the richer the details will become.

Visit your dream destination frequently for a few minutes at a time – while brushing your teeth, making a coffee, loading the laundry – and you will be surprised and delighted by what is revealed.

As your day unfolds, deeply authentic insights and ideas will come to you when you least expect them, when you are relaxed and consciously focused on other things. So carry your travel log with you. Keep it beside your bed. *Expect to be inspired!*

If you're right on track...

Does 'dreaming big' always result in a radical reset of career in the short term? No, absolutely not! In most cases, my clients discover that their dream destination is simply the bigger, bolder and more beautiful version of *the path they are already on*. There is a recognition that, at a deeper unconscious level, they already knew what they wanted:

- 'Ah, that's why I opted for that role!'
- 'Ah, that's why I was so keen to experience working overseas!'
- 'Ah, that's why I turned down that move!'

Looking back, they can see that their life and career decisions were guided by an undercurrent of authenticity that they hadn't consciously recognised. Although this guidance was outside their conscious awareness at the time, they could see with hindsight that it was there all along – nudging, cautioning, inspiring them forwards with every choice they made.

In such cases setting out towards your dream destination is relatively straightforward. There are no major course corrections required. Rather it is a matter of recognising 'you-shaped' opportunities right where you are. It does often invite a courageous resetting of ambition, leaning into what's truly possible and unleashing your authentic potential. But this rarely requires an immediate resetting of roles and relationships. Rather, it is a moment of decision, a conscious commitment to get out of your own way and go for it.

If this is true for you, wonderful! You can acclimatise to the scale of your dreams gradually over time. And the rest of this book will help you chart the terrain you're in, find the guides who can help to show you the way, and make progress as swiftly, sustainably and productively as possible.

If another path is calling you...

But what if this is *not* true for you? What if, as you consider who you really are and what you really want, a dream destination begins to emerge that suggests a completely different track to the one you're on?

This was the case for one of my clients, in a group finance role, who discovered that her dream destination involved shifting the passion projects she pursued outside work to the centre of her work and her life. Her passion was her love of dogs. She retrained and launched a dog-grooming service, which she ran successfully for 12 years before retiring. This enabled her to continue her volunteer fundraising work for a greyhound rescue charity of which she had long been an enthusiastic supporter. She shifted from making a living to making a truly authentic life.

If a dream destination is calling you onto a very different path, then a more significant course correction may be required, but even then you don't need to make a change straight away. It *might* be achieved through a fairly rapid transition – one that could involve retraining or further study, a significant sideways move or even a temporary step back – as I did when my 'early midlife crisis' prompted me to leave behind my career in engineering and retrain as a development consultant. But such a radical shift is not always necessary, possible or even desirable. If you have significant family or financial commitments – or if you'd simply prefer a gentler transition – your course correction might be best achieved through a more gradual series of intelligent, enjoyable, strategic moves, perhaps beginning with just a modest renegotiation of your current role. Even if it seems like your current starting point is less than ideal, you can move towards where you want to be from wherever you are. And if your dream destination is a goal with soul, you'll find joy on every stage of the journey.

And if your dream destination has triggered your inner protector into a frenzy, how do you decide between your current well-paved and familiar route with the safety it seems to provide, and the growth, contribution and inspiration of your most authentic adventure? And, if you choose to commit to your new dream destination, how do you get out of your own way and go for it?

In Chapter 11, I will share an approach that will help you dissolve your dilemma. It has been my own personal experience, and the experience of the many clients I have guided through this process, that once you have all your thinking out into the open, a clear preference is found. One of the options will 'feel right', and it may not be the one you imagined when you started. Yes, I have seen clients unravel what was holding them back from making a bold move on to something completely new. But I have also seen many discover that the opportunity was there all along to create something new and far more authentic, right where they already were – no move required.

For now, it is enough to recognise that any tension or discomfort is showing you that it is time to make some kind of change. Recognise you don't have all the information you need yet, so open yourself up to reading the signs and signals inside and out. When you ask your inner protector and your inner adventurer to work together, you dismantle the internal barriers of belief, and allow your most authentic path to emerge.

Let go of the pressure to make a decision. Instead, allow yourself to settle into the process of deciding. And, as you do, use everything you've discovered so far about who you really are and what you really want to make the most of where you are now.

Bring your whole self to your work and your life today and, instead of grasping for an immediate answer, simply stay with the question.

Watch, listen and feel for the guidance that comes through.

Trust yourself to find a way

If you follow the steps and suggestions above, the chances are you'll rendezvous with a vision for your career and your life that is beyond anything you've previously allowed yourself to imagine. Whether it is the bigger version of what you were already creating – such as a senior role in your current organisation or industry – or something completely new makes no difference to the impact of discovering your dream destination. Immersing yourself in this authentic vision for your work and life is likely to trigger a heady mix of excitement and terror. You may ask yourself, 'Could I really do *that*?' This is the meeting place of your inner protector and your inner adventurer.

When the voice in your head says, 'But what if it all goes wrong?', be sure to make space for the part of you that says, 'But what if it all goes very *right*?!'

Growth and contribution are two sides of the same coin. You have not yet become the fully realised version of you that you can see at the heart of your vision. But pursue your dream and you'll grow as you go. The 'you' that reaches your dream destination will have been transformed by the journey. The 'you' that arrives will not be the 'you' that sets out. Remember, both skill and self-confidence grow from regularly doing things we're not certain we can do.

The time has come to shift from following a one-size-fits-all preset path to becoming the authentic leader of your own life, the intrepid explorer you were born to be. And if your dream destination is bigger, bolder and more beautiful than anything you've ever previously imagined – so awe-inspiring that it's almost too astonishing to imagine – excellent! Remember, you are a living, breathing miracle, deserving of a career and a life that you love. You are unleashing your potential for even greater contribution and, in the process, creating the even more magnificent version of you. The vision you have for yourself – the authentic and flourishing 'you' at the heart of a life that you love – is big and bold and beautiful. This vision serves you *and* it serves the world. And you'll be dedicating a chunk of your life and the gifts you've been given to this authentic adventure.

The most important question is not 'Am I worthy of this journey?' but 'Is this journey worthy of the *real me*?'

Commit to the journey. Trust yourself to find a way. Trust yourself to learn what you need to learn, to meet who you need to meet, to find the resources you need to find. That is the way all true adventures unfold. One small move at a time. One discovery at a time.

And that's how much of the specific guidance you need will come. Just like the satnav on your car, giving you one small but perfectly optimised next move at a time. Remember, it's absolutely fine to not have the specifics clear yet. An authentic and inspiring direction of travel is enough for now.

Spotting the treasure along your trail

As you navigate the next few days and weeks, pay attention to what pops up in your awareness. Long-forgotten memories of the past, new ideas for the future, a moment of recognising the brilliance of someone else. These are the previously unnoticed reflections in your rear-view mirror, possibilities on the horizon, the brilliance reflected back to you by those in your wings. The pipeline of inspiration is now open, and the real you knows you're listening.

What can you look forward to from here?

- ✦ Your *inner satnav* will guide every move you make.
- ✦ Your *autopilot* will take care of every new skill and strategy you learn.
- ✦ Your *cruise control* setting will allow you to find your flow and make progress enjoyably and, at times, completely effortlessly.

Didn't know your mind–body vehicle came 'factory fitted' with an inner satnav, an autopilot and even a cruise control setting? Not surprising, given that none of us got the manufacturer's instructions! So, before you head out on the open road, it is my pleasure to introduce these little-known features, enabling you to more fully harness their extraordinary power. Welcome to the missing owner's manual for your incredible mind–body vehicle.

PART THREE
Your Incredible Mind–Body Vehicle

10. Listen to Your Inner Satnav

Follow your bliss, and don't be afraid, and doors will open where you didn't know they were going to be.

– Joseph Campbell, mythologist, from 'Joseph Campbell and the Power of Myth with Bill Moyles' (1987)

The miracle of satnav

Many years ago, when our children were small, my husband gave me an unexpected gift. We were about to take a family holiday in Devon, a rural idyll of twisting country lanes a six-hour drive from our home in the north of England. 'I know it's not your birthday yet,' he said, with a twinkle in his eye, 'but you might want to open your pressie...'

When I did, I found myself holding some kind of gadget and, at the risk of sounding ungrateful, I confess that my heart sank. Over the years, my well-meaning and generous husband had gifted me a string of gadgets for which I had no real need, and which languished long forgotten at the back of a cupboard. Little did I know how differently this gift would play out. This gadget was my first ever satnav.

Now if you learned to drive recently and your GPS-based satnav system is built into your phone or the dashboard of your car, you may be thinking 'Wait! What? Satnav used to be a separate device?' Maybe you've never had the experience of navigating a complex route without the assistance of a guidance system. In which case, the significance of this moment may not be immediately apparent to you. For me this gift was life changing. You see, the truth is I am seriously 'navigationally challenged'. I am naturally poor at finding my way around. In fact, pre-satnav I used to visit the same destinations over and over again and still get lost. And that's why a system that showed me every move I needed to make to reach my destination was a revelation.

Now, I'll admit, it took me a while to incorporate this guidance system into my driving habits. I had to learn to glance at the images *and* listen to the voice, integrating these data sources into my decision-making in real time. I had to develop my sense of timing so that I made my moves at just the right moment. Most importantly, I had to learn to trust the source of the guidance I was receiving, trust that I was being offered the optimal route, even when I thought I knew better. But as I did, my whole experience of driving was transformed. I was shocked to discover that routes I had been taking for years were actually far from optimal. I discovered shortcuts and fast tracks and far more enjoyable routes – less crowded, more scenic and easier to navigate. And as I leaned into this guidance, following the nudges I received with ever-increasing confidence, I learned how to relax and enjoy the ride.

It wasn't long before Jayne – the voice of my first satnav – became my absolute favourite travelling companion. Not only did she provide clear instruction, she was there to assist me when things went wrong. When I misinterpreted her guidance, there was no criticism or complaint, no heavy sighing or long silence. She simply recalculated my optimal route, and shared her revised guidance. Even when I took a complete dead end, she let me know I was off track, advising me in her calm, dulcet tones to simply 'turn around when possible'.

As others indulged in satnav rage, complaining about rare and fleeting misdirects, I revelled in the peace and calm of this astonishing new experience. I felt like I was in safe hands. Over time, I found myself increasingly willing to embark on journeys into completely unfamiliar territory. Even routes I'd avoided based on their reputation for being barely navigable inspired nothing but curiosity and a sense of adventure. Hello, Spaghetti Junction, Birmingham! The experience was so *freeing*, it transformed my experience of driving. It felt like a little real-life miracle.

It wasn't long before I found myself wishing there was such a thing as 'satnav for life'. Wouldn't it be great if we could receive guidance from a trustworthy source at every twist and turn in our careers and our personal lives? How wonderful would it be if we could tune ourselves to totally personalised, judgement-free guidance on every decision, big or small? And then I discovered that we can. The incredible mind–body vehicle you were gifted for this journey came fitted with a state-of-the-art *inner satnav*.

Your satnav for life

Back in Chapter 6, I invited you to make a 'you-turn' – to reclaim your journey by discovering and honouring who you really are, and to commit to creating and experiencing your most authentic life. Authenticity is the key to effortless, enjoyable and sustainable success. But making a you-turn is not a one-time deal. It is an all day, every day process of turning to your deep, wise self for guidance.

So, as you get ready for your authentic adventure, let's take a closer look at the incredible guidance system you have available to you 24/7 – your inner satnav for life. In the pages that follow, you'll discover how to tune yourself to the guidance you receive and incorporate it as you drive for results. You'll learn how to clear any interference that makes your satnav signal unclear, and even how to dissolve full-blown dilemmas, so you always know which way to turn. Let's begin with a brief recap of the key principles we've explored so far.

True authenticity begins with recognising that, beyond the conscious thinking human personality that you think of as 'you', there is a deeper, wiser, soul-level self that is the *real you*. As you mindfully and deliberately cultivate a connection with this soul-level self, you activate a channel of communication between your conscious mind and your unconscious – your human ego and who you really are. In any moment where you make this deep inner connection first, you allow your soul to shine through your personality. You put your best self, your true self, in the driving seat. In doing so you gain access to an endless stream of insights, energy and encouragement – everything you need to drive for your dreams and thrive as you drive.

Listening to your inner satnav involves looking to the real you – the truest, deepest, wisest, soul-level aspect of yourself – for guidance. You find your authentic choices, and your most meaningful and magnificent career and life path, when you're willing to ask yourself one simple yet powerful question:

'What would the *real you* do?'

Then do it. Even when the guidance you receive is surprising. Even when you're not sure how this phase of your journey will unfold. Even when you're guided to make a move that diverts from the fast tracks and well-paved superhighways followed by others.

This is not easy at first. When you've been trained to look outside yourself for answers, learning to trust yourself and your own authentic impulses can be awkward and unsettling at first. Breaking away from a well-worn route that represents the norms of your profession, or the norms of the organisation you work for, can trigger your inner protector into a tirade of objections. But as I discovered when I first embraced the gift of satnav, magic happens when you're willing to trust and follow the unique real-time guidance that you're being given.

Recognise that your soul-level self, like a satellite system far above, has a perspective on your journey that your brilliant but limited conscious mind cannot yet fully access. Trust that there is a bigger picture to any guidance you receive. And remember that you don't need to receive all the details of your journey all at once. You may catch glimpses of that bigger picture, a map of the landscape you're being guided through. But, just like the satnav in your car, your inner guidance system will often give you *just one move at a time*. And that's all you need.

You can navigate even a lifelong journey, and reach your ultimate destination, one beautifully optimised move at a time.

Now there is one small catch, one which explains why so few of us access and act upon the authentic guidance we receive all day every day. Unlike the satnav in your car, your soul does not speak English. The guidance you receive is not presented as a series of clearly articulated, easy-to-follow, specific spoken instructions. Why? Because the real you has been communicating with you since the day you were born, long before you acquired language, long before our human species even developed language. Your soul speaks a language that is beyond words, so it will take a little practice to tune yourself to this guidance and learn to interpret its signals.

The good news is that, like the satnav of your car, your *inner satnav* is easy to access when you know how. Welcome to the simple yet profound guidance of your emotions.

Tune into your truth

Your emotional guidance is the easiest to access because it is always present. All day every day you are *feeling something*. Whether you are aware of it or not, whether you're paying attention or not, emotional guidance is available to you 24/7.

In the absence of any official owner's manual for this state-of-the-art satnav, we've all had to try to understand our emotions based on the instructions we've received over the years – and across the generations – from other human beings. Some of these unofficial guides were well intentioned, authentic and emotionally well adjusted. Others were battling, in crisis and hanging by a thread. This leads to a mixed bag of ideas and beliefs about human emotions, and the part they play in a life well lived.

For example, you may have been conditioned to believe that some emotions (the good-feeling ones) are 'positive', while others (the not-so-good-feeling ones) are 'negative'. It's easy to see where this idea comes from. We instinctively know to move away from pain and towards pleasure, and the structures of the human brain and nervous system are designed to help us do just that. But if, like most people, you have been encouraged to embrace the good-feeling emotions and to avoid the uncomfortable ones altogether, you've inadvertently been trained for a world of trouble.

Seeing fear-based emotion as something to avoid leads you to want to escape any uncomfortable feeling – sadness, anger, anxiety, guilt, shame – as quickly as possible, without learning or benefitting from its appearance in any way. Depending on the culture you were raised in, you may even have been taught that some emotions – such as anger – are unacceptable, and should not even be felt, let alone expressed. Over time, you begin to anticipate feeling difficult emotions and the desire to avoid them can become so intense that anxiety kicks in. You feel afraid of feeling fear.

The mental and physical thrashing around we do in an attempt to avoid our difficult emotions is often the very thing that keeps us spinning or stuck.

That's because the feelings you have *about* your feelings can hook you into a fear-driven loop, with one fearful thought leading to the next and the next. Over time, self-criticism and self-doubt become the norm, fuelled by the feelings you have about your unwanted feelings – feeling guilty for feeling sad or disappointed, feeling embarrassed for feeling anxious or envious, feeling ashamed for feeling angry or depressed. The story in your head that says 'some emotions are acceptable and others are not' will scramble your authentic guidance every time.

Before jumping into how you can unravel these distressing emotional loops, let's set some core principles in place. If you did have the owner's manual for your amazing mind–body vehicle, what might the satnav chapter actually say? Based on both the latest research in positive psychology, and the consistent themes from wisdom literature penned since the dawn of civilisation, here's what we know so far.

The way you feel in any given moment is not a reaction to your situation. It's your body's response to *the thought* you are *thinking* about your situation.

As each moment becomes a minute, and the minutes flow into hours, the thoughts you think string together into stories. This near-constant internal narrative of the situation you're in is never true in the absolute sense. It is just one take on your current situation, your life so far, and your prospects for the future. Your emotions are feedback from your body, letting you know *how accurate and valid your story is*. As you learn to tune into this feedback, and steer your thoughts and your actions in accordance with the guidance you receive, your emotions will show you what your deepest, wisest self knows to be true.

Feel your way forward

My own understanding of how this emotional guidance system works in practice draws on the work of many teachers and authors, but I wish to particularly acknowledge the extraordinary work of Esther Hicks and its contribution to my own journey of discovery.

Want to know how you can feel your way forward in every moment as your most authentic path unfolds? The clues are in a game my sisters and I would often play as children, one you may well have played yourself. We called it the 'Warmer, warmer' game.

To begin, one of us would silently choose an object in the room as a target, and another had to guess what they'd chosen. The 'guesser' would turn on the spot or move slowly around the room. The 'chooser' would guide them by saying, 'Warmer' or 'Colder' as they moved closer to the target object or further away. If the guesser got close to the target, the chooser would excitedly say, 'Hotter. Very hot. Scorching!' until the object was correctly identified, and the game began again.

So it is with your inner satnav. The thought that the real you is thinking in any given moment – your deepest, broadest, highest truth – is the target. You scan your environment and think thoughts in response to whatever you notice. Those thoughts are your best guess at the truth – your perception of reality based on partial data, your conditioned beliefs and your experiences from the past. The gap between these two thoughts – your deeply authentic soul-level truth and your perception in this moment – is known to you by the way you feel. If the thought you are thinking as a conscious personality – your guess at the truth – is close to the thought that the real you knows to be true, you will experience the blissful harmony of internal alignment. The closer the alignment, the more delicious the feeling. And as you deliberately steer your mind in the direction of the best-feeling thought you can find, you lock on to your authentic homing beacon – an ever-present signal that can guide you forward and onto your most authentic path.

Your emotions let you know in every moment the gap between 'you' as a conscious, conditioned personality and who you *really* are. Your mission, should you choose to accept it, is to continuously minimise that gap.

And as you do, stress gives way to the first glimmer of hope, which paves the way for optimism, enthusiasm and eventually the bliss of flow. You feel energised, expansive and fully alive – like the whole of you is pulling in the same direction. And that's because it is.

Turn around when possible

It is with this insight in place we can see that even our most challenging and uncomfortable emotional responses are, in fact, powerful *guidance*. Challenging emotions are not merely an inevitable part of the human experience which must be avoided or endured. They are signals letting you know your ego-based thinking has strayed far from your own deep truth. Uncomfortable emotions let you know your perception of reality – the story you're telling yourself about your past, your current situation, or what's possible from here – is a million miles from the story your soul would tell.

Even the most distressing and deeply uncomfortable emotional responses offer invaluable guidance to help you realign with who you really are and what matters most to you. They are intended to be helpful, not harmful. They are messengers letting you know a course correction is needed, letting you know you are focused on what you *don't* want instead of what you *do* want. They are your inner satnav saying, 'Turn around when possible.'

So it is possible to feel your way forward. You can play the 'Warmer, warmer' game in every given moment. You can pay attention to how you feel, notice how closely aligned you are in this moment with what your deepest, wisest, soul-level self knows to be true, and correct the course of your thinking if need be. You can reach for a thought that feels just a little bit better than the thought you were just thinking, and you can feel the immediate feedback that lets you know you have come into closer alignment with who you really are. You can task your inner protector with monitoring how you feel and flagging for your conscious attention anything that feels off to you. You can unleash your inner adventurer towards your bravest, boldest, most meaningful and high-contributing adventures. You can be fully present here and now to the most magnificent aspects of the life that you've already created *and* feel the untapped and unlimited potential of the moment, the more that is possible from here.

This real time guidance from your own deep self allows you to drive for your dreams and thrive as you drive.

So, now you know how to tune into your satnav and interpret the emotional guidance you receive, a new question arises. How can you ensure that the signal is as clear and strong as possible, and tune yourself fully, so you *can move forward with courage and confidence?*

11. Boost Your Signal Strength

If we are only half in our bodies,
we are only half in our truth.

– Julia Cameron, *The Right to Write* (2017)
Author and screenwriter

Clear the interference

Fear-based emotions such as anxiety, anger and shame are *noisy*. The sensations are intense. The energy crashes around your body. Your guts feel like they're spinning, and your heart is clamped in a vice. Your inner protector works hard to get your attention. And you don't need me to tell you that if you ignore these emotional signals, they often get much louder.

Love-based emotions, on the other hand, are often quieter and more subtle, at least at first. It's not easy to catch the quiet whispers of hope and optimism when you're in and out of waves of anxiety, anger or overwhelm. That's why it's so important to clear the interference, to soothe and quieten your mind and body, so that the guidance you are continuously offered can truly be received.

The first key to clearing the interference is to let go of the well-trained habit of judging your feelings as right or wrong. Stop sorting your emotions into columns labelled good and bad, positive and negative, acceptable and unacceptable. See the full spectrum of emotional responses as simply the honest reaction of your body to the thoughts that you're thinking. Let whatever you're feeling be OK.

Support yourself through any wave of difficult emotion by replacing self-criticism with self-compassion. Allow the emotion to be what it is, perhaps observing and labelling it to create a little distance: 'This is anxiety' or 'This is sadness'. And as the wave of strong emotion rushes through you, speak to yourself as you would speak to someone you love.

You'll soon discover that individual waves of emotion and sensation last only for 45 to 60 seconds. You'll have experienced this already with the wave of laughter that's triggered by a great joke. It rises, it peaks and it ebbs away. Any emotional response that lasts longer than a minute or so is being fuelled by a story, and by the feelings you have *about* whatever you're feeling. In other words, it is a whole series of waves in response to individual thoughts that blend one into the other, creating the ongoing intensity of an enduring state. Letting go of judging your feelings as right or wrong allows you to be present, to get the message, to embrace the story if it inspires and empowers you – 'I am strong. I am capable. I can do this!' – or changing it if it doesn't. With a little practice you can *choose* the soundtrack of your own mind, shift out of the loop created by the fear of feeling fear, and settle into the moment.

Reality-check all warning signals

The second key to clearing the interference on your satnav signal is to understand that the emotional response of your body barely distinguishes between a threat or opportunity that you *actually observe* or one that you *vividly imagine* – as you may have discovered when watching a scary movie.

That can be an incredibly empowering asset if what you're imagining is aligned with who you really are and who you're becoming, allowing you to be energised by your dream long before you arrive. But it can be problematic if you react to every warning offered by your inner protector without first testing it against reality and what your deeper, wiser self knows to be true.

You can be triggered into your stress response in a fraction of a second. Perceptions of threat, thoughts of actual or imminent danger, travel the fast pathways in your brain designed for your survival. And, as we explored in Chapter 4, it can take considerably longer to switch back again from fear mode to love mode, refocusing away from what you don't want and towards what you do want, reclaiming your awareness that all is well in this moment. But switch back you must, and as quickly as possible.

Much of what your body responds to is imagined and not a here-and-now reality. Recognising this gives you the chance to mindfully feel your way into the more subtle, wiser, more authentic guidance beneath. It creates the space in which you can make finer distinctions about what your inner satnav is actually telling you. For example, if you find yourself swinging between excitement and terror ahead of a high-stakes presentation, slow down and pay attention to your stream of thoughts. You may notice that you are running two mental movies – one of success and another of disaster. The terror you feel when you imagine disaster is not a here-and-now mortal threat, but an imagined scenario to which your inner protector has attached potentially significant consequences. It's important not to dismiss the imagery out of hand, since imagery is the second language of your guidance system – more on that in a moment. Instead, it's invaluable to explore the scenario for seeds of truth. By allowing the mental movie to play, but viewing it as a more impartial observer, you are likely to make much finer distinctions about what you're really being shown. And this in turn may spark ideas and actions aligned with bringing your best self forward – being well prepared for your presentation, rehearsing rather than merely planning, and perhaps requesting pre-meetings or mentoring conversations with one or more of the participants ahead of the big day. If you stay with the emotional guidance you're given instead of trying to push it away, then examine the thoughts that underpin the emotions, you'll make discoveries that will allow you to create incredible results and enjoy the ride.

Silence the static

The third and final key to clearing the interference is to find healthy ways to quieten and soothe any sensations in your body as much as possible. As you know, physical sensations are not solely driven by emotional responses. Discomfort can be caused by a myriad of sources, including;

- sleep deprivation
- hormonal imbalance
- overly tight muscles
- inflammation
- food intolerances
- any undiagnosed or unaddressed medical issues.

If your body is chronically uncomfortable, this creates a level of background noise that acts like static on the signal from your inner satnav and makes it much harder to discern the authentic guidance you're given. If you're acclimatised to your body feeling a particular way, you may tune out these chronic sensations, like the hum of your fridge that you don't hear until it clicks off. And that means you may not be aware just how good it is possible for your body to feel, or how extraordinarily nuanced your authentic guidance can be.

Many years ago, I discovered how profound an impact this chronic background noise can have without even being recognised. I decided to run an experiment in which I would temporarily cut all refined sugar out of my diet. In general I was eating healthfully, but between meals I had a habit of using a sweet snack as a pick-me-up during an afternoon energy slump – or even just when I felt a little bored. I wanted to reset my habits and was curious to see what impact the change would have.

You probably already know a sugary 'fix' creates a temporary high that is followed by an energy crash and an accompanying sensation of agitation that can then drive the need for the next fix. It took three days for my conditioned sugar cravings to pass completely, but when they did, my body suddenly went quiet. I felt incredibly peaceful. In the days and weeks that followed, I realised that much of the near-constant, low-grade agitation I had felt for years, and acclimatised to as 'going with the territory' of being a busy working mum, was in fact my body's reaction to sugar. Slaying the sugar dragon felt like I was instantaneously on the other side of another ten years of personal development. I felt calmer, more confident and more present than I could ever remember. And I could hear more clearly than ever before what my body was trying to tell me.

Take a few minutes now to scan your body from head to toe for areas of tension or discomfort of any kind. Tap into your still power, move the spotlight of your attention slowly and *notice what's really there.*

Ask yourself what's needed to release any discomfort. What small changes could you make in how you nourish yourself, rest or gently stretch your tight muscles?

And is there anything going on that you've been ignoring for a while, hoping it'll just go away? Is it time to book in for a check-up with your doctor or other healthcare provider, just as you would take your vehicle in for a service and an MOT? Listen to the truth and honour any insight or impulse that arises.

Take action now to take care of the one precious vehicle you've been gifted for this lifetime. Not only will this reduce the risk of you breaking down, waylaid at the side of the road. It will also remove 'static' from your satnav signal and support you in more clearly and confidently feeling your way forward.

Over time, you will become more consistently aware of how you feel, tuning into your body rather than tuning it out. As you commit to listening to your inner satnav, and to act on the guidance you receive, you'll become increasingly adept at knowing your own deep truth, able to confidently navigate even the most uncertain situations with enthusiasm and grace. Where you once found yourself going round and round in circles you will now make real progress, guided and energised by the lightness, the expansiveness, the pull of your most authentic choices. Your best 'next move' will almost always be clear.

When you meet a fork in the road...

The joy of knowing you have uniquely personalised and utterly reliable guidance available to you 24/7, and the sense of clarity and confidence that awareness inspires, are just the beginning of the transformation you'll experience. New connections, new information – the right person or resource coming into your life at just the right time. Magic happens when you let your soul guide your steering.

Yet from time to time you may hit what feels like a major crossroads, and when you do it might not be immediately obvious which way to turn. It may appear that your satnav is glitching out as you experience very mixed feelings about the choices before you. The two roads unfold in your mind's eye. Both have a powerful pull. Both also feel risky in their own different ways. You may feel paralysed by indecision. And in the absence of an authentic decision to proactively make a change, you'll most likely stick with what you know.

No decision becomes a decision by default.

But here's where things get particularly interesting. If a new possibility is truly authentic for you – such as the dream destination you identified in Chapter 9 – then the opportunity to make a change will present itself over and over again. Though you may continue moving forward at speed, you'll feel the relentless whole-body tug of the exit from your current well-paved route, the slip road to a new way forward that speaks to you every time you drive by. Your dream destination becomes the idea that won't go away.

Navigating dilemmas such as these can be both invigorating and intensely stressful. This is because *both* of the potential routes forward have significant merit: either one would meet some of your deepest and most authentic needs and desires, but seemingly at the expense of others. For example, even if the pull is towards a new opportunity with your current employer, your hunger for the excitement, challenge, growth and other rewards of a fresh challenge may be in conflict with your desire to be loyal to your current boss or team, and the security, familiarity or status of your current position. If you wish to move forward with ease and joy, such dilemmas cannot be ignored. They must be actively dissolved.

When you don't know which way to turn

Begin by noticing the tendency to frame our major life decisions as just two options. 'Stay in current role' or 'Pursue something new'. 'Have a great family life' or 'Have a great career'. 'Be employed' or 'Be entrepreneurial'. These are false dichotomies! It is entirely possible to pursue something new right where you are, to renegotiate the scope of your current role and pursue something new part time, or to pursue something new with a group of your existing colleagues and contacts. It is entirely possible to have a great family life *and* a great career, to find wonderful childcare support, to work part time, to go freelance. It is entirely possible to be employed *and* to be entrepreneurial, to bring innovative solutions to current customer challenges, to initiate new product and service lines, to make the business case for launching and leading a new business unit. Your dilemma will begin to dissolve the moment you commit both your head and your heart to the task of generating additional personalised possibilities, new options that take society's old, conditioned highways to happiness – corporate employment, entrepreneurship, full-time parenthood, etc. – but which go beyond the limits of those rigid well-worn routes. You create truly authentic options for yourself by first recognising and owning *all* your genuine heartfelt desires.

You pave the way for new inspired ideas by first letting yourself want everything you genuinely want.

A more authentic approach to dissolving the dilemma is to *avoid compromise and instead optimise*. This involves flushing out all your needs and aspirations – both those that are inspiring you towards making a change and those that are holding you back. If you feel you are at any kind of crossroads right now – big or small – take out your travel log, and work through the following process. This will dissolve your dilemma in three simple steps.

Step 1: Open your travel log to a new page, and divide it into two columns. Give each column a heading that represents one of the two options you

can see, the choice you have been wrestling with. This might be as simple as 'Stay' and 'Go'. Or it might be far more specific, for example;

'Continue to invest in ____________ [current technical specialism]' and 'Carve out new career in the field of ______________ [new field of interest]'

'Recommit to my current relationship' and 'End things and make a fresh start'

'Refresh our current home and connect more fully with our community' and 'Create a new life in ____________ [new location]'.

Whatever headings you choose, ensure that both titles are stated in the positive. For example, if you're fed up with your current job role and feel like you're stagnating, it's not helpful to your authentic evaluation to label that left-hand column with 'Settle for the job I've got'. Instead, remember that your dream destination is not only an external set of circumstances, but also an *inner state of being*. Ask yourself what words best represent you staying with your current employer *and flourishing*. For example, 'Refresh and reshape my current role and career direction with ____________ [current employer].'

Listen to your back seat drivers

As you consider the choice before you, notice that each of these options has its advocate, a back seat driver with an exciting-but-scary story to tell. If you slow down and listen, you'll hear the case each advocate makes. For example, let's work with 'Refresh current role' or 'Take new job'. The part of you that thinks you should take the new job may say things like, ‘You’ve outgrown where you are. It’s Groundhog Day here. The people are great, but you’re not learning much of anything new. You’re stagnating. That new project will look fabulous on your CV. You’ve always wanted to work on something like that. It’ll stretch you. You’d be crazy to turn this opportunity down, and you’ll regret it if you do.’ Conversely, the part of you in favour of staying right where you are might say, ‘You are doing so well here. You’ll be up for promotion soon, and you’ve been given the nod for senior leadership in the long run. Do you really want to throw all that away after everything you’ve invested? The economy is so uncertain, and you have bills to pay and a generous pension and people who are counting on you. It would be selfish to put all that at risk. You’d be crazy to leave right now, and you’ll regret it if you do.’

Step 2: Take another look at the options before you. Tune yourself to the voice in your head that advocates for each course of action. As you listen to the story each tells, capture the specifics under the relevant heading – not as pros and cons, but simply as *key points of the narrative*. Ping pong back and forth between the options, following along as each advocate interrupts the other. Listen to their stories. Get their thoughts on paper. Let both parts of you have their say.

You may find that as you consider your options, an insight arises as a negative consequence rather than a benefit in the first instance. For example, 'going for it' may feel risky, or staying where you are may feel limiting and dull. In these instances, turn the insight around by asking yourself, 'What is the opposite of this for me?' For example, if 'going for it' feels too risky, then notice that you associate safety with staying where you are. This may or may not be your safest option in reality, but your reflections are showing you your internal *barriers of belief*. Similarly, if staying with your current employer feels limiting and dull, you may associate growth and excitement with going for it elsewhere, where in reality, growth and excitement can be found wherever you decide to cultivate them.

Invite your inner team to work together

Once you have a complete first draft of your two columns, you are ready to move on to the next step. This is the point at which you invite your inner protector and your inner adventurer to work together for your highest good. How can you fully live your most authentic adventure and make progress as safely and sustainably as possible?

Step 3: Take each point in turn and *fully consider*, 'How could I meet this need while pursuing the other option?' For example...

- 'How could I manage and mitigate the risk of moving to a new role employer/starting my own business/entering a new field?'

- 'How could I build the network of contacts who could help me to make this transition?'
- 'How could I stretch myself, learn and grow right where I am?'
- 'How could I refocus and re-energise my current role, to meet more of my authentic criteria and increase my enjoyment and job satisfaction?'

And now look again at your options. Read back everything you've written. As you do it may well be that you suddenly have a strong sense of your most authentic way forward, a whole-body 'yes!' to one option or the other. Perhaps you realise it is absolutely the right time to move on or perhaps you realise that the new possibility was an ego-driven shiny distraction, and what you really want is to refresh, reinvigorate and recommit to your current role and career path.

As you tune to the option you most genuinely desire, you're likely to find that there are valid points in the two narratives that do indeed need to be addressed, such as the need to save a financial cushion before moving on or the need to renegotiate your role with your line manager. But in the light of a truly authentic decision, those are simply aspects to manage, and you can develop an action plan to do just that.

Sink into your awareness of what matters most to you, your deeper resonance with one option over the other. Let yourself want what you most authentically want.

Now, if you embrace the most authentic and compelling option, does that mean that the journey will *always* be easy, carefree, and joyful? No, of course not. Life is inherently unpredictable and uncertain. Whatever route you choose, you're likely to hit bumps in the road. You may even meet insurmountable roadblocks that get in the way of the *full* realisation of your dream. But if you are pursuing a goal with soul, and loving the journey, then even a partial success can be the making of a great life.

As you cast your mind forward to the end of your career, or even the last days of your life as a whole, consider now what is necessary for you to be able to look back without regret. Moving forward with no absolute guarantee of success takes courage. But, as is often said, 'In the end, we only regret the chances we didn't take, the relationships we were afraid to have, and the decisions we waited too long to make.'

**Whatever happens along the way,
it's far easier to live with 'Ah well...'
than 'If only...'**

So how can you maintain this essential perspective? How can you go beyond even the magnificent emotional guidance of your inner satnav, and tap into your authentic impulses even more fully and easily? Wouldn't it be great if your inner satnav actually could be a voice in your head and your heart, guiding your every move – a genius-level co-driver keeping you safe, supported and on track while you make progress like a pro?

Your future self as co-driver

I first learned about the role of a professional co-driver decades ago when my husband – a fan of motorsport of any kind – introduced me to high-speed rally car racing. The first time I watched was a televised stage of the

National Tour, his favourite course, Grizedale Forest. My heart was in my mouth as I watched some of the best drivers in the world tackle mud-slicked dirt tracks, narrow tree gaps and hairpin bends at astonishing speed. There were heart-stopping moments as they slid round corners narrowly missing boulders, tree trunks and occasionally spectators. But I was hooked. How did they seem to know exactly how deep the ditches were, whether to drive through or drive around? How did they have such foresight about what was waiting for them around each corner? In short, how did they know *exactly what to do and when*?

My husband pointed out to me that the driver was not alone. Each had a co-driver – a clipboard-carrying source of moment-by-moment guidance. 'They scout the course in advance and write it all down,' he told me. 'The instructions they're calling out tell the driver what they need to know – where the hazards are, as well as the chances to pick up speed. It sounds like a foreign language, but the co-driver knows what's coming and shares it in a kind of code. The driver gets all the glory, but it's a team effort.'

You too have access to someone who can offer you that same level of specific, totally authentic guidance for *your* adventure – a pro who's already scouted, and then completed, the course you're about to take. That someone is your *future self*.

Your authentic future self – the 'you' that you see at your dream destination, the evolved and thriving version of you – is not, in fact, rooted in the future at all. They are here now. The fact that you can envision them – see them in your mind's eye, hear them and recognise them as you at your brilliant best – shows you that they are already in you and available to you. What you're seeing is how you *already* show up in your most authentic moments. Your future self is just the consistent expression of that brilliance, the thriving and flourishing version of you that you are becoming as you break through your internal barriers of belief.

Your authentic future self is who you're becoming by more fully expressing who you really are, and by letting go of who you are not.

And that means that you can cultivate a relationship with this aspect of you. Instead of watching them from a distance, hoping you'll one day 'meet', you can be with them now, and ask for any guidance you need. You can even have a conversation, and in the course of that dialogue, ask any questions you have about your best way forward from here. Your authentic future self used to be where you are now. And you'll soon discover that they're excited to share what they learned along the way.

Scouting the course

I'm well aware that this sounds strange, but it works. And I'm not asking you to take my word for that. I invite you to find out for yourself.

Take a few minutes now to slow down and, hand on heart, tap into your still power. Envision your dream destination, and settle in for a chat with the 'you' that you find there. You may find it helpful to close your eyes and allow the conversation to unfold. Or you may prefer to reach for your travel log, and write down your questions, waiting in a curious and open state before writing down your answers. Pause, listen and learn.

As with all things, the more you connect with your future self and ask for words of wisdom or encouragement, the easier it gets. And if your experience unfolds as it has for me (and for every client I've suggested this to, and who was open-minded enough to give it a whirl), you'll soon have the strange but validating experience of asking for guidance and getting quite a different response to the one you expected to get. And if you follow the guidance you receive, you'll be pleasantly surprised – perhaps even astonished – by what happens next. I've now lost count of the number of times I've been guided to pause before doing something that I thought I *should* do, only to receive a nudge a short time later to go ahead and to subsequently discover my timing was impeccable. This part I can't explain, but I know it to be true in my own direct experience.

So set aside a little time for this dialogue each day. You're envisioning your dream destination anyway, so why not stay for a chat? You'll soon find yourself driving as part of an incredible team, with real-time guidance when you need it, even when you're moving at speed. Not a bad return on investment for a few minutes a day.

At this point, you may be wondering why I spent so long talking about 'feeling your way forward'. If authentic guidance can be received just by connecting and conversing with your future self, why introduce emotional guidance at all? The answer is simple but vitally important. Noticing how you feel is the only way you know you're talking to your *authentic* future self – who you really are at the soul level, expressed in human form – and not your 'idealised' future self, the polished and perfected person you were trained to become. Guidance from your authentic future self will always feel kind, encouraging and inspiring. Even guidance that helps you learn from any trips into the chaos zone will be delivered with compassion and wisdom, never as harsh criticism. It is the powerful combination of internal dialogue and emotional awareness that lets you know you can trust what you're being guided to do next.

And as you increasingly trust and follow the guidance you receive from your future self – knowing that the actions are inspired at a soul level – it won't be long before the change is visible to others. It's not just that you'll be energised, clear minded and authentically confident. It's that you'll increasingly take consistent action in areas that previously required willpower and self-discipline, because now you've got *soul discipline*!

Your true self is in the driving seat. Your future self is guiding you. You experience the thrill of honouring your deepest desires and inner harmony as your satnav feeds back that you're fully aligned, bringing your whole self to the moment. You value any detours for the discoveries they bring. What may well look like self-discipline to others will soon feel to you like simply the most authentic, nourishing and inspiring choice available.

Self-discipline is what you do to yourself. Soul-discipline is what you do for yourself.

Driving for joy

You've already shown yourself to be dedicated, ambitious, willing to do whatever it takes to get results whatever the cost. So, ask yourself, what would your life look, sound and feel like if you applied the same drive and ambition to loving here that you were trained to bring to 'getting there'?

A commitment to feeling good – optimising your quality of life by improving your internal emotional landscape – is a commitment to optimising your mindset. Quality of life flows from quality thinking.

When your thinking is expansive, possibility focused and generous, you show up as your true self, your best self, the 'you' that gets phenomenal results *and* loves the journey. Locked on to your authentic guidance, the essence of your emotional life will be an undercurrent of love: appreciation, enthusiasm, optimism, excitement, passion, peace, hope, playfulness and joy.

When you're no longer willing to tolerate the intolerable, you learn to treat your willpower as a reserve tank, For Emergency Use Only. You draw on your willpower as a survival strategy, supporting yourself through intensely challenging moments in the chaos zone, and then doing the work of insight and alignment on the other side, setting yourself up for a different experience next time. When you refuse to accept anxious achievement and the validation of others in place of authentic success and happiness, you create the joyful and sustainable experience you deserve, and you stay true to the unique and authentic contribution you were born to make.

Feeling good is not just a 'nice to have'. It's what lets you know you're on the right track, allowing the *real you* to shine through.

Feeling good throws the channel of communication between you and the *real you* wide open, so you can benefit from the never-ending streams of ideas, inspirations and solutions. It's what sets you on a course of growth and contribution that makes for a richly rewarding and deeply meaningful career and life, a life where happiness is not a destination but a way of travel.

The incredibly exciting news is that, when it comes to making effortless and enjoyable progress, your inner satnav is just the first of the *three* key assets you have at your disposal. Allow me to introduce the second, your amazing autopilot.

12. HARNESS THE POWER OF YOUR AUTOPILOT

Between stimulus and response there is a space.
In that space is our power to choose our response.
In our response lies our growth and our freedom.

– Viktor E. Frankl, *Man's Search for Meaning* (1946)
Austrian neurologist, psychiatrist and Holocaust survivor

Introducing your amazing autopilot

Have you ever driven a familiar route home and then realised that you don't remember driving? If you've been driving for a while, the chances are it's happened not once but many, many times. It's a disconcerting experience the first time, when you realise with a jolt that you weren't paying full *conscious* attention to the task at hand. 'Was I a danger to myself and others?' But you soon realise that this experience was not a case of dangerous distraction. On the contrary. Some part of you – an incredibly clever part – *was* paying attention and making all the tiny adjustments necessary for your ease, comfort and success. You dabbed the brakes and pressed the accelerator whenever needed. You took every tiny twist and turn of the road with ease. You found your way to where you wanted to be, automatically and effortlessly. You were in a driving trance, a state of *flow*.

As a learner driver, I found it hard to imagine being able to drive without paying conscious attention to every single move. Driving is such a complex skillset. From learning the basics of how to stop, start and steer to more involved elements such as manually changing gear, I soon got the hang of operating the vehicle itself. But from the very first lesson I realised this was just the beginning. I had to learn to manoeuvre the vehicle – reversing around corners, three-point turns, parallel parking. But even more challenging was learning to do all this on a road network shared with other road users – practising full 360-degree awareness, mirror-signal-manoeuvre, interpreting the endless stream of signs and markings. I memorised the *Highway Code*, so I knew and understood how everyone is *supposed* to drive, only to discover that's often not how people drive in practice. So I learned to manage and mitigate risks so that I could drive safely regardless of the moves of those around me.

All this felt exciting but also somewhat overwhelming at first. I was lucky enough to learn to drive in a vehicle with dual controls and was immensely grateful that I could take responsibility for the vehicle gradually and in stages. But over time, and with practice, small actions clustered and coalesced to become *automated skillsets*. The moves involved in handling the vehicle itself become second nature, and I was able to dedicate almost all my conscious attention to my surroundings, navigating whatever terrain presented itself. Even at this stage, having passed my driving test, I still remember being incredulous when a friend asked me to change the radio station. How exactly was I supposed to do that and drive? But the clustering and coalescing continued as more and more of the moves I made – repetitively and with intense focus – were programmed in as automated strategies, then handled by my unconscious mind: full conscious involvement no longer required. Eventually the experience became one of *ease and flow*, and occasionally of 'driving without driving' – the ultimate experience of effortless success.

Now imagine for a moment what your experience of *life* would be like if you could fully harness this powerful process in support of your effortless success in other areas? What if you could move towards your dream destination with automated success strategies in play, habits that support your wellbeing as well as your productivity? What if you could let go of much of the effort involved in getting results by releasing outdated habits that no longer serve you? What if you could free up your conscious attention and energy for challenges that move you forward and increase your capacity to contribute in future, such as solving complex problems and upgrading your skills? In short:

What if you could harness the full power of your autopilot, so it could take you to where you want to be more easily and enjoyably than you ever thought possible?

It can be done, and the pages that follow will show you how.

Your autopilot programming

Your autopilot is already playing an active role in your life, and that's a good thing. Imagine getting up in the morning and having to figure out from scratch how to use your toothbrush, how to dress and how to operate every door handle. You'd never leave home. You benefit all day every day from these and many other routine matters having been delegated to the care of your unconscious mind.

What's more, it's not only mundane behaviours and decisions that are automated under your current programming. *Everything* you do superbly well is supported by automated strategies deployed on your behalf by your unconscious mind. Beyond the complexities of driving your car and navigating your route, you may well have other activities you excel at, such as playing a musical instrument, speaking a second language or playing your favourite sport to a high standard. You're likely to be aware of these examples because you can remember the hours and hours of practice involved in attaining your current standard of excellence. And if the particular activity was *your choice*, much of that practice will have been joyful, inducing the exhilarating altered state known as 'flow', the trance state that athletes describe as being 'in the zone'.

How did you develop these complex skills to your current level of competency? How did you acquire the mindset, skillset and muscle memory needed to be able to automatically achieve what was once completely beyond you? In the same way as you learned to drive: insight, focus and practice. You saw how it was done, you focused your full attention and you practised repeatedly until the skills and strategies were also yours.

So how and when does your autopilot kick in? And how can you harness this powerful process and apply it deliberately, to accelerate and enhance the skills and strategies you want to cultivate from here?

Your unconscious mind tracks everything to which you give your conscious attention, looking for patterns. It notices what you're most interested in, takes this as being important to you and gets busy helping in any way possible. Whatever you pay conscious attention to is prioritised for further attention, and other seemingly less relevant stimuli tuned out. The intention is that you'll be able to focus more fully and concentrate more easily. If an experience is repeated, or if it is attended to with enough intensity, your unconscious mind will then take this as a particular priority and flag to you anything in your surroundings which is the same or even just similar. You may have experienced this phenomenon if you've ever decided to buy a car and focused on your preferred make and model, only to start seeing it everywhere.

If the relevant neural pathways are repeatedly stimulated, the brain literally reshapes itself in response to this stimulation, in a process known as neuroplasticity. In a matter of weeks, your brain lays down a fatty sheath around the relevant neural pathways. This sheath increases the speed with which electrical impulses can travel that pathway, turning a faint track in your brain into a fast track, and eventually a mental superhighway. These fast tracks are then used in preference to other neural pathways in an effect known as the expediency bias. That's why we have habits of thought as well as habits of behaviour. Your mind shapes your brain (neuroplasticity) and then your brain shapes your mind (expediency bias). It's a never-ending loop of automation designed to give you more of whatever you focus on, faster and more easily than ever before.

Where Your attention goes, energy flows

Now isn't that a wonderful thing? Your unconscious mind will give you more of whatever you focus on, with no conscious effort on your part. It's like the genie in Aladdin's lamp saying, 'Your wish is my command.' But it's *only* a wonderful thing if you're focused on something you want.

Your unconscious mind will give you more of whatever you focus on, whether you want *it* or not.

You've been trained by your caregivers, teachers and bosses to search your surroundings for anything that is *not* as you'd like it to be. This allows you to spot problems – current or potential – with the positive intention of solving or preventing them. But your unconscious mind tracks this interest and says, 'You want to notice things that are not good enough? I can help you with that', and flags for your conscious attention everything else that is *potentially* problematic, while simultaneously blinding you to everything that is going well. Cue anxiety, stress and eventually overwhelm.

In such moments, it can seem like your mind has a mind of its own. But this is not self-sabotage or some kind of 'inner demon'. It is simply your unconscious mind doing what it is designed to do:

- taking direction from your conscious mind about what matters most
- prioritising whatever you pay attention to for further attention
- automating the whole process as fully as possible.

As Aladdin himself discovered, even with an all-powerful genie, you still have to be careful what you wish for.

Detours, ditches and autopilot glitches

So, you didn't have an owner's manual. And that means you've accumulated a plethora of fear-based responses to anything that looks potentially problematic. Your current autopilot programming is almost certainly a mixed bag of strategies – some supportive of your progress, others distracting from and delaying your authentic journey.

The good news is that none of this programming is permanent. No matter how long you've been thinking or behaving in ways that are not true to who you really are, you can 'debug' your autopilot, letting go of any strategies that no longer serve you. Glitchy, unwanted and outdated programming can be updated and overwritten. You can free yourself from unwanted and outdated habits, replacing them with more authentic choices that can become as effortless and automatic as your old reactions used to be. And in so doing, you can come into alignment with who you really are and the life you want to live.

Sometimes you only know you've got an autopilot glitch once you find yourself already nose down in a ditch. You're driving along, happily ever after, and then *boom*:

- Someone crosses a line, and you're triggered into an angry rant.
- You see that crucial presentation pop up in your diary, and a wave of panic courses through your body.
- You overhear a cruel comment about your weight, and bury your face in a bucket of ice cream with a side order of shame.

Confronted with such an unwanted habit, you may wish you could hit 'Restore to factory settings'. After all, how are you supposed to make a change if you're already doing the thing you don't want to do by the time you realise you don't want to do it? But 'Restore to factory settings' is not an option any of us have, or would ever really want. Most of your automated strategies are healthy and helpful. Walking, talking, eating, cooking, writing, calculating, emailing and an endless list of your current strengths are underpinned by your existing autopilot programming, an infinitely complex collection of effortless success strategies you'd never want to wipe clean. Instead, we can bring *selected* strategies back into our conscious awareness – the habits of thought and behaviour that most often take us off course – and debug from there.

If you've ever tried to change long-standing habits, you know how hard it can be. I sometimes ask my audience members to raise their hand if they've ever set a New Year's resolution and not achieved it. Every hand goes up. But now you know how your autopilot works – taking whatever you focus on as a request for more of the same – you understand the importance of focusing on what you do *want* to create and experience, and not what you want to avoid. And that's the main reason why so many resolutions fade almost as fast as the New Year's Eve fizz. Most resolutions are focused on what you want to quit, get rid of or lose – smoking, drinking, debt, excess weight – instead of what you do *want* in your life as a result of making the change – energy, health, vitality, financial freedom and abundance, a good-looking, good-feeling healthy body.

Your first task then is simple: focus on purpose. Keep your eyes on the prize of your dream destination and selectively sift your current surroundings for a match. Notice what is already as you would wish it to be, and scan for opportunities to move forward on your most authentic path. Minimise the amount of time you spend focused on problems by getting the data you need about what you want to change, and then turning as swiftly as possible to face in the direction of what you want instead. Continually steer your attention towards what you want.

This may be simple, but it's not always easy, at least not at first. As we explored in Chapter 4, there's an adverse camber on the road, thanks to the negativity bias. That bias is made up of priorities hard wired into your nervous system, as well as the soft-wired conditioning you received since birth. Your inner protector makes good use of your autopilot system in support of its primary aim: keeping you alive. But with a clear vision of the life you want to create and experience for yourself, and a willingness to focus in that direction as consistently as possible, you can reprogramme your autopilot to take on this risk-management and refocusing task too. You'll soon be surprised and delighted to find that, while those around you respond in alarm to any perceived threat, you swiftly assess the situation, then turn your attention from the problem to potential solutions.

So, if you're experiencing unwanted detours, ditches and autopilot glitches, it's time to make a change. Now is the time to take full ownership of your amazing autopilot, and harness its power in support of your authentic success. You are so much more than just 'the programmed one'. *You are the programmer.*

Programming on purpose

Your first role as the programmer of your own autopilot is to identify a particular opportunity for change. This is most easily achieved from the relaxed 'observer' position we explored in Chapter 4 – clear minded, objective, connected to the *real you*.

It might be tempting to go straight for the biggest opportunity for change – the one habit of thought or behaviour that, if changed, you believe would make the biggest difference to your work and life. But if something comes to mind that feels hugely overwhelming, I recommend that you park that for now. Note it down in your travel log, along with any other major changes you'd like to make over time, and identify something *small but significant* as a warm-up. The approaches that follow absolutely work for the big stuff too. In fact, it's when making the biggest changes that matter most to you that the information that follows will be most crucial – if you want to *enjoy* the process of change, and maintain that change for the long haul. But, just like when you learned to drive, it can be fun and exciting to get a feel for your vehicle first, and enjoy picking up scale and speed with practice. Choose something that you know would make a difference to you and beyond you, but which can be a short-term practice ground for the skills and strategies we're about to explore.

What is the one *small* habit of thought or behaviour that, if changed, would make a positive difference to you and the people you care about? Consider how you've reacted in the past. Begin to imagine *how you want to respond instead.*

Refocusing from your unwanted reaction onto your preferred future response is crucial, as it creates a vision for your success that your unconscious mind can then help you to create. The language of your inner satnav is *emotion*, but the language of your autopilot is *imagery*. It is the *images* that you imprint onto your unconscious mind that become the reference point for future automation.

World-class gymnasts know this. They pause and mentally rehearse the perfect execution of their routine. This connects them back to countless hours of practice in the safety and familiarity of their own gym, activates their nervous system to execute the moves and creates a singular point of focus that induces flow, putting them in the zone.

Visualising success imprints upon the unconscious mind a precise blueprint for excellence.

Focus on your desired destination

Let's take as an example the experience of chronic exhaustion. You decide you're sick and tired of feeling sick and tired. You decide you're willing to make some small changes that you know will make a big difference. But, not knowing that your autopilot is fluent in imagery, not English, you say to yourself, 'I'm going to stop *staying up late*. And to do that I'm going to cut out the *mindless scrolling* by staying away from my *phone*.' Notice that, even though those statements are all negated, what your unconscious mind sees in the accompanying *imagery* is 'staying up late', 'mindless scrolling' and 'phone'. You want more of that? You got it!

Instead, begin by imagining yourself waking in the morning wide eyed and refreshed. See yourself rising from bed with a slow stretch, a smile on your face and a spring in your step. Run a mental movie of yourself making the aligned choice of going to bed at a reasonable time, leaving your electronic devices elsewhere. See yourself smiling and feeling good about that decision. Your incredible unconscious mind will embrace your request, and nudge and support you in your desired direction.

And this translation is true of *any* instruction you receive, whether it's a thought of your own about what to do next or a request from someone else. If I ask you right now, 'Please, whatever you do, *don't* imagine a baby crocodile wearing a red bow tie' what happens? You *have* to imagine the baby crocodile and his snazzy red bow tie, just to understand what I've asked you *not* to do. You can't focus on something you *don't* want and arrive easily and comfortably where you *do* want. Your autopilot will keep you stuck by giving you more of what you don't want, not because it doesn't want you to succeed, but because – through the power of your focus – that's what you 'asked for'.

Keep your travel log to hand and, for the next few days, pay attention any time you experience even a shimmer of discomfort from your inner satnav. Notice the fear-based thoughts and accompanying imagery. Then turn it around. Get your eyes back onto the road ahead by asking yourself, 'What is the opposite of this old way of reacting for me?'

- Feel a little wave of anxiety as you spot a looming tight deadline? Notice the shift in how you feel when you *imagine* making a quality contribution on time, if not early.
- Feel too tired at the end of the day to enjoy your evening? Translate 'I'm exhausted' into '*I could do with more energy*' and notice the impulses that arise to stretch your body and breathe more deeply.
- Feel sad and frustrated that your cancelled train kept you from your family? Recognise your true desire for connection and quality time, and notice the loving impulses that flow when you *imagine* a heartfelt and loving reunion when you get home.

Over time, as you become increasingly attuned to the subtle signals from your satnav, you'll become more and more aware of the fear-based 'away from' messages in your own self-talk and in the environment around you. I recently took a lift in a tall office building and saw a safety notice that read, 'In the event of an emergency, don't panic.' The slightest shimmer of discomfort and I was mentally rewriting the notice to say, 'In the event that the lift stops unexpectedly, remain calm.'

Pivoting your focus in this way helps you connect to what it is that you really do *want*, which may be something to create over time or may even be something that's available to you right here right now. So, the next time your boss calls a meeting and says, 'Let's not take too long over this', translate it to, 'Let's make this brief and productive.' Practise this pivoting and condition it in and, before you know it, you'll be *pivoting on autopilot*.

Each day, as you visit your dream destination in your mind's eye, see yourself as the thriving and flourishing person you will become as a result of making the change you identified above, and many other inspired and authentic 'course corrections'. Enjoy switching between two perspectives, and note what you experience from each:

- ✦ seeing yourself in the picture, as though watching a home movie
- ✦ seeing your dream destination as if you are already there, taking in the scene through your own eyes.

Shift between these two perspectives, and enjoy the subtle richness that comes from both *seeing yourself there* and *being there*.

Programme in your desired destination, and let your autopilot work *with* you. That's how you get *the whole of you* driving in the same direction.

Accelerate the automation

Now you have a clear vision for who you are becoming, and the new pattern of thought or behaviour you want to experience. You may have heard various declarations as to how long it takes to change a habit – anywhere from 21 to 60 days, depending on which research you read. But that's how long it can take without an understanding of how your autopilot actually works. You can accelerate the process, so your new choice becomes a habit as quickly as possible.

Almost a decade ago, I had an experience that brought home to me just how quick and easy – and fun – it can be to embed a new habit. It was a grey and frosty morning as I drove my youngest daughter Emily, who was about 11 years old at the time, on the 15-minute morning run to school. Suddenly, she called out, 'Cheese on wheels!' Startled and confused, I replied, 'What...?!' Emily turned and pointed, and in my rear-view mirror, I saw the bright yellow car that had just passed us by. Cheese on wheels.

A few moments later, Emily called out again. 'Cheese on wheels!' she squealed in delight, pointing at a small yellow van in the supermarket car park. 'That's two-nil! Come on, Mum!' And that's when I realised this was a *game*, and my sneakily playful daughter had a head start.

For the rest of that journey, and again on the route back home that afternoon, my daughter – able to give the game her full undivided attention – left me behind in a cloud of dust. But the next day we were more closely matched, and as we scanned our surroundings, we giggled and squealed and argued about what shade of yellow (not orange!) we were allowed to count.

And then it happened. On the third morning, I shouted out 'Cheese on wheels!' ... *after* I'd dropped her off at school.

It was so automatic it was as if someone else had said it. And I shouted before I'd even *consciously registered* the yellow car. I laughed out loud.

Why am I telling you this story? Because it showcases all *three* of the factors you can use to accelerate the automation of *any* habit or strategy you want to embed.

The first factor is *repetition*. Repetition is of course the bedrock of any kind of practice. But it's easy to fall into the trap of thinking that becoming proficient in a skill or changing a habit takes a certain amount of time. It doesn't. It takes a certain amount of *repetition*. That's why you can learn to drive with a few months of lessons for an hour or two a week, or on an intensive course where you take your test at the end of the week. Knowing this, you can accelerate the automation of your new strategy by visualising your successful execution of the habit over and over throughout the day. In a coaching session, for certain new thought paths – for example, shifting from being terrified of standing up in front of a sea of faces and speaking, to being excited and energised by the opportunity – I'll condition in the change at least five or six times there and then, to help my client get off to a flying start.

The second factor is a combination of *rhythm* and *rhyme*. Now, I know 'Cheese on wheels' isn't exactly poetry, but my unconscious mind loved its rhythm and rhyme. This is something all great teachers know: even tiny children can learn abstract concepts like the alphabet if set to the tune of 'Twinkle, Twinkle, Little Star'. So come up with a little mantra that reminds you of your new choice, one that has enough rhythm and/or rhyme to be catchy.

For example, some years ago, I wanted to engage more readily in courageous conversations, including giving more honest and direct feedback, but found that my old programming about not hurting people's feelings was keeping me from a relaxed and authentic exchange. To help me get out of my own way and make the change, I adopted as a mantra a quote from shame researcher and advocate of 'daring leadership' Dr Brené Brown (2015): 'Clear is kind.' It did the job. And this simple mantra still pops into my mind occasionally, if I'm at all tempted to be 'nice' instead of authentically loving.

The third factor is *intensity of focus*. Why did my daughter get the hang of the game faster than I did? Because she could give it her full and undivided attention. I, on the other hand, had to give my attention to the road and all the other road users, and not exclusively to searching for bright yellow cars. As we laughed and exchanged playful banter, we became even more engaged in the game. The intensity of our focus, and the feel-good emotions it inspired, made this simple experience truly memorable. Just two days later – and around an hour's total practice – the automation was complete. And all these years later, wherever I go, it's still the yellow cars that stand out.

Have fun along the way

So now it's time to put this new information about your state-of-the-art autopilot to good use. You have a clear vision of your success, seeing your authentic 'future self' thinking aligned thoughts and taking inspired action. Consider how you can factor in greater *repetition*, by coming back to your vision several times throughout the day, perhaps by associating it with something else you know you'll be doing, such as making yourself a hot drink or taking your dog for a walk. What catchy little phrase can you use to anchor yourself to this powerful vision, one with *rhythm* and maybe even a little *rhyme*? You might pop this phrase on sticky notes and put them on the fridge, the bathroom mirror, the edge of your computer screen – anywhere you're sure to see them often – or perhaps set it as a series of reminders on your phone to prompt you at random times throughout the day. And finally, when you focus on this vision of your successful change, give it as much of your attention as you can. Be as single minded as possible, bringing *intensity of focus*, and zooming in on the aspects that intensify the feel-good emotions that let you know you're facing in the right direction and you're on your way.

Then you get to be surprised and delighted when everything unfolds effortlessly and enjoyably. You find yourself making aligned choices with ever-increasing ease. And you begin to see that you are surrounded by opportunity. The opportunities were there all along, but – like the 'Cheese on wheels' – passed you by until you knew what you were really looking for. When you make the change fun, you make the change stick.

13. ACTIVATE YOUR CRUISE CONTROL

Whatever your work may be, think of your work as a channel for the expression of mind and soul... you will soon receive from within all the power and inspiration you could possibly desire.

– Edmond Szekely, Creative Work: Karma Yoga (1973)
Hungarian professor of psychology

Debug your code

Now that your vision of your success is clear, and you are beginning to harness the power of your autopilot, you will experience the joy of alignment far more of the time. You'll experience moments of flow with increasing frequency, letting you know that the whole of you is pulling in the same direction. The first few days of making any new change will require deliberate conscious focus – mindfully redirecting your attention towards the outcome you want – in order to accelerate the automation. Thankfully, your new behaviour will soon be as automatic as the old problem behaviour used to be.

Until then, as you navigate the early stages of the change you have chosen, remember to listen to your inner satnav guiding you towards *the most aligned option* available to you in any given moment. Authentic actions always feel good after we've taken them, and not just before or during the activity itself. So while the old habitual choice may seem easier upfront, thanks to the expediency bias, nothing compares to the overall pleasure and meaning to be found in making the aligned choice – especially if you *celebrate every little win*. Catch yourself being brilliant. Cheer yourself on, as you would a great friend. Bring that feel-good emotional intensity to reinforce the change.

Now it's important to acknowledge that, as you navigate those early days of the change, there will be times when you'll still be triggered by something outside your awareness, causing the old behaviour to play out. It was seeing this time and again as a newly qualified coach that sparked my curiosity regarding the workings of the unconscious mind and led me to train as a hypnotherapist. I wanted to understand why brilliant and dedicated people would leave a coaching session enthused and inspired to make a change, clear on the one small action that would make the biggest difference, and then come to the next session having not maintained their clear, *self-determined* priority. Sometimes sheepishly apologetic, and at other times bullishly defensive, they rationalised that they were 'just too busy'. But as the changes often focused around saving time and effort, most would then admit that they simply didn't understand why they hadn't made the change.

As we've already said, the first you know about any misaligned autopilot programming may be when you find yourself already nose down in the old familiar ditch. In these moments, instead of getting upset with yourself or the situation, slow down and breathe. Recognise such experiences as life showing you the glitchy code that still needs to be debugged – the transformational work you haven't done yet.

Remember, your evolution is about progress, not perfection.

Find the trigger

Accept that whatever has happened has happened – apologising and making amends later, if appropriate – and get curious about what you can learn from the experience, to create the potential for a different experience next time.

Bring to mind a recent experience where you felt triggered into an old, unwanted pattern of thought or behaviour. What did you see or hear in your environment that set the old pattern in motion?

- ✦ a disapproving 'look' on someone's face?
- ✦ a pleading request or demand for help?
- ✦ the sight or smell of your favourite food?

If you're not sure at first, slow the mental movie of that moment *right* down. Tap into your still power – relax and stay curious. You may initially be blind to the specific trigger, but with the help of your unconscious mind, you'll soon have full conscious awareness – and with it the chance to reintroduce freedom and make a fresh choice.

Now, as the programmer, you have a *specific* opportunity to clean up your code, accelerate the change and make it stick for the long haul.

Bring the specific trigger to mind, and ask yourself, 'If I could respond to this *in any way I choose*, how would I *want* to respond?'

- ✦ How would you want to feel?
- ✦ What would you want to say to yourself?
- ✦ How would you want to behave?

Now visualise yourself responding in that new, more authentic way. Mentally rehearse your new response. Use repetition, rhythm and rhyme, and focus with intensity on the new behaviour and the good feelings it inspires.

Very soon, you'll have your first experience of avoiding the ditch and staying on track. You may experience a hairy moment as you skid quite close to the edge, but with your hands on the wheel and your eyes on the prize you'll get yourself back on track. Phew! The next time, you'll see the ditch and feel a tug on the steering wheel, but you'll drive on by. Before you know it, you'll be driving on and simply enjoying the scenery.

Debugging and automating these tiny choice points – such as how you respond to disapproving looks or demands from others – is the key to making change stick for the long haul. It can even be fun. And your unconscious mind, clearly imprinted with imagery of your authentic success, will generalise these changes into other areas which you didn't even realise were related. For example, if you clean up how you respond and relate to your boss or other senior colleague, so that your conversations are more of a respectful meeting of equals, you're likely to find yourself responding differently to other authority figures in your life. It's exciting to suddenly catch yourself automatically responding effectively and authentically in situations where you haven't even done any conscious change work. How's that for effortless success?

With just a little practice, this awareness of the functioning of your autopilot and its accompanying change processes can be applied to any change you want to make. This includes the 'big stuff' you may have identified and parked earlier. And remember, big doesn't necessarily mean big for anyone else. It could simply be that the change really matters to you, so it has a lot of emotional intensity. This might be learning to perform a crucial aspect of your work role under intense pressure, such as our earlier example of delivering a high-impact presentation in a high-stakes meeting. Or it might be something more personal, such as responding in a kind and compassionate way towards someone – a child, your partner, a colleague, or even a complete stranger – who is not being kind towards you.

Get out of the ditch, then pave the new path

Expecting yourself to debug your autopilot in the precise moment when you've already been triggered into an unwanted response is too much to ask. It's only once you have regrouped, and reconnected to who you really are, that you'll have access to the wisdom and insights needed for authentic, sustainable change. That's when you can be truly honest with yourself about what happened. Not harsh. Not unkind. Just honest. And this means staying present to the moment, or at least returning to it as quickly as you can – no denying, no excusing, no numbing the uncomfortable feelings with food, drink and gossip. And no pretending that 'everything is fine' when it's not.

There's no value in sticking a smiley face sticker over an engine warning light, an avoidance strategy known to psychologists as toxic positivity.

Feel your authentic feelings and receive the messages they bring. Then you can focus on forward motion by making your next inspired move, and committing to pave a new path so you can experience the same trigger differently in future.

So, the next time you experience a setback and find yourself triggered into an old unwanted pattern of thought or behaviour, give yourself a chance to reconnect on the inside first.

If you're already in an intense fear response – panic, shame, rage, etc. – then the fastest way back to your true self is to do something physical.

This might be standing up and walking or running. When you move your body, you move your mind. But if that's not possible, take control of your breathing. First, simply become aware of your breathing, which will bring you into the now – not the re-runs of the past (what just happened) or the projections of the future (what you're afraid will happen next). Then gently regulate your breathing towards a sustained rhythm.

When triggered into an intense stress response, you may find the following two-step process to be helpful:

- **Square breathing** – Think of breathing in, pausing with full lungs, breathing out and pausing with empty lungs as four sides of a square. Count to four on each side as you inhale – pause – exhale – pause. This will take you out of the fight or flight response.
- **Blowing out the birthday candles** – Inhale deeply and quickly, and then exhale slowly, just as if you were blowing out the candles on your birthday cake. When you are in love mode your out-breath is naturally longer than your in-breath. Doing a few deep breaths where you extend the length of your out-breath shifts your body closer to that 'rest and digest' state, soothing the emotional centres of your brain and allowing your full, clear-minded thinking to come back online.

If you're willing to practise these breathing patterns occasionally, a few times a day for a few days, you'll create the muscle memory that comes with *focus, rhythm and repetition*. With that you'll create a fast track in your physiology from your stress response into the calm-but-alert state that is optimal for you to address any challenge, and make an authentic decision about what to do next.

Remember, it's not so much what happens, but how you *respond* to what happens that really determines how things unfold: whether you are triggered into a brief detour or stay much longer than you would wish nose down in that ditch of despair. It's the feelings you have *about your feelings*, and the harsh stories you tell yourself *about yourself*, that create the toxic loop that can keep you stuck. So practise regulating your breathing and your self-talk. See setbacks and detours as an inevitable – and potentially useful – aspect of your most authentic adventure.

You're on a never-ending journey of discovery, and sometimes the *discoveries are on the detours.*

Now you have the most crucial chapters of the missing owner's manual for your incredible mind–body vehicle. You know how to listen to your inner satnav, recognising that your emotions are not random physiological responses, but your body's feedback regarding your alignment with who you really are. You also have insight into the workings of your incredible autopilot, understanding that you get more of what you focus on, whether you want it or not. You know to 'be careful what you wish for' – focusing in the direction of what you do want to create and experience – and also how to debug any glitchy programming so you can move more consistently and enjoyably in the right direction.

So, let's take what we've explored and apply it back to your overall dream destination. How can you harness the power of your autopilot to help you stay focused in the direction of your most authentic adventure?

Choose your own scenery

We've already explored the power of visiting your dream destination – envisioning your future success and happiness several times a day. There is fun, energy and inspiration to be found in consciously connecting with this vision frequently and with focused attention. But we also now know your autopilot is paying attention to *everything* you see, hear and feel – whether you are paying conscious attention or not. That's why we can sometimes be triggered into autopilot strategies by nudges that are outside our conscious awareness – an effect put to good use by advertisers, politicians and social media platforms wanting to get your attention and influence your choices. And that means there is a wonderful opportunity for you to further automate your alignment with who you really are and what you really want, by surrounding yourself with triggers, reminders and nudges of your own.

One fun and powerful strategy is to create a vision board. This is a collection of images representing different aspects of your dream destination, placed where you'll see it frequently throughout your day. This might include images relating to:

- vibrant good health
- loving relationships
- career and financial success
- bucket-list experiences of things you'd love to see and do.

> Your vision board can be a physical corkboard covered in photographs and clippings from your own life or downloaded images – anything that represents whatever you want to create and to experience here and now more fully. Or it could be a virtual board, perhaps set as your screensaver image, so that it's there on your computer every time you return to your screen.
>
> Every time you see your board, you are imprinting your autopilot with the vision of your authentic, enjoyable and sustainable success.

Once you have a collection that inspires and energises, you can also print out extra copies of some of the images and place them around your environment, perhaps considering where their particular nudge might be most useful. For example, if your vision includes images suggestive of vibrant good health, you might post a few on the front of the fridge, a kitchen cupboard and the door of the wardrobe where you keep your exercise clothes. And if there is one photo that's the most powerful of them all, one that truly represents authentic success and happiness to you, why not make it the home screen image on your smartphone and the screensaver on your computer? These images will act as unconscious cues, nudging you towards your most authentic choices all day every day, and eventually and enjoyably towards your dream destination.

Activate cruise control

And that's when the magic truly begins. As you embrace the authentic guidance of your satnav, and harness the power of your autopilot by creating a more supportive environment – inside and out – moments of effortless alignment become more frequent and longer lasting. You will increasingly find your way into *flow* – that blissful state where all you have to do is steer and almost everything else can happen automatically. This is *cruise control for life*!

Having access to cruise control isn't the same as a self-driving car. You still have to keep your eyes on the road and steer. But travelling at speed on cruise control – freeing up most of your conscious attention, so you can make effortless progress *and enjoy the ride* – is thrilling, life-giving and joyful beyond measure. Researchers consistently report that the amount of time spent in flow is one of the most reliable predictors of their test subjects declaring themselves to be happy.

Now nobody drives on cruise control all the time. It's not realistic, and perhaps not even desirable. Overcoming challenges in an authentic and meaningful way is part of the richness of life. But if you can strip out the struggle, you'll be able to achieve even more than you ever thought possible. Your old conditioning may occasionally chip in that 'If it doesn't feel like hard work, you're not working hard enough'. But making a difference is about the value you add, not the suffering you endure. There will be plenty of genuinely tricky terrain to navigate on your most authentic adventures. There's no need to seek it out or to make things any harder than they need to be.

Let's take a closer look at how you can activate your cruise control setting – cultivating the conditions under which you're most likely to access this blissful state of flow. I'll share the techniques and strategies that will give you even greater access to your inner guidance and your amazing autopilot, enabling you to automate your authentic excellence even more fully. And we'll explore the transformational shortcuts that can help you make progress more quickly, sustainably and joyfully than you ever thought possible.

Turn still power into your superpower

If you're ready to set yourself up for effortless and authentic success, it's time to turn still power into your superpower.

Take a closer look at the lives of great thought leaders from history, those from any walk of life who you most deeply admire, and you'll find that many incorporated a daily practice of deep stillness. This typically involves a dedicated time of day to slow down and turn one's attention inwards. It offers the chance to drop into a deeper, more authentic and expansive aspect of oneself, and the vastness of whatever the individual believes to be beyond themselves – God, the universe, the quantum field. This practice of turning inwards for guidance and peace of mind goes by many names – daydreaming, meditation, prayer, contemplation, self-hypnosis. Each features its own rituals and each has its own emphasis. But all have one thing in common: accessing the altered state of consciousness known as trance.

In this state, you are at your most highly suggestible – a fact put to good use by hypnotherapists who can help clients create changes almost within minutes with which they may have struggled for months or even years. Trance is an altered state in which the gateway to your unconscious mind is wide open, and where reprogramming can take place with little or no conscious interference.

Now if your inner protector is starting to get a little twitchy, concerned that we're veering into territory that is a bit too 'out there' or even just off topic, remember that we've already established one key fact:

Trance is a state you already access *naturally* and frequently throughout your day.

It is the state you are in when your autopilot guides your behaviour without any conscious involvement on your part – even complex tasks such as driving home without paying attention to the mechanics of driving. It's the state you move through as you drift off to sleep at night and rouse again the next morning. And it's the state you are in when you daydream during pleasant but routine activities, such as enjoying a hot drink or taking a shower, or when you become so absorbed in an activity that you lose all track of time.

Cruise your way to inspired ideas

Trance is the name we give to the state you're in when information can flow most freely between you and the *real* you – and, depending on your world view, perhaps also all that is beyond you. Trance is the state when your autopilot is most suggestible, which makes changing habits, retaining material when studying for exams and automating new success strategies far faster and easier. It's also why being in trance helps you receive guidance and inspiration. Have you ever taken a shower and suddenly had a brilliant breakthrough idea come to you seemingly out of nowhere? The gateway is wide open in both directions.

The best way to boost your transformation is to boost your trance formation.

This means deepening your dialogue with your authentic future self. Making requests of your body for healing or pain management. Asking for help, from the whole of you and beyond, in dark and difficult moments. Connecting to endless ideas and solutions. Accessing trance on purpose – and *with purpose* – is the basis of self-hypnosis, and it's easy when you know how.

This was a secret known to the prolific inventor Thomas Edison. At the time of his death in 1931, he had an extraordinary 1,093 patents to his name. Though he is perhaps best known as the inventor of the incandescent electric lightbulb, his inventions spanned numerous fields including electric power storage, telephony and sound recording. When asked the secret of his seemingly endless creative breakthroughs, Edison would say it was his habit of taking frequent naps. But look a little closer and you'll see his true 'secret'.

Standing under a banyan tree in the Edison & Ford Winter Estates in Fort Myers, Florida, you'll find a statue of Edison. In the left hand of the aluminium statue is held a polished steel ball. This is a nod to Edison's practice of taking his 'naps' in his office armchair holding a steel ball in each hand, allowing his hands to rest above two metallic bowls. He would focus on the challenging problem he was working through and relax towards sleep, with the expectation of receiving insights and optimal solutions. He was not interested in the sleep itself, but in the *trance* state he would enter along the way. If he relaxed too far and entered the deeper sleep state, his hands would relax and release one or both balls, causing a crashing sound that would wake him again. He would grab his notebook and pencil, and immediately record any ideas, images and impressions that had come to mind. Genius!

Fast-track your trance

So if you wish to access the trance state, on purpose and with purpose, the key is in encouraging your body to swiftly and deeply relax into a state close to sleep, while your mind stays awake and aware. In a light trance, such as the relaxed alert state you're in when studying an interesting subject, your brainwaves slow just enough to drop into a pattern dominated by *alpha* waves (frequency around 8–12 Hz) – a peaceful, attentive and receptive state of mind that's well worth cultivating as your normal way of being. Drop into deeper trance, and you reach theta dominance (4–8 Hz) – the deeply relaxed, inwardly focused daydreaming state, ideal for problem-solving and creative thinking, and from which you may emerge with no recollection of time passing. Drop further still and you reach delta dominance (0.5–4 Hz) – for most people the sleep zone, but for practised meditators, the realm of transcendent experiences, free consciousness and oneness with 'all that is'.

There are several small adjustments you can make which will accelerate your access to trance and stabilise you once you get there. If you have limited time before there's somewhere else you need to be, set an alarm to wake yourself, so that you can relax fully and deeply now.

Take a few minutes now to deliberately experience the trance state. Consider asking someone to slowly read these steps to you, or record them on your smartphone. Read them slowly, pausing for

30 seconds or so between each step.

- ✦ Relax in a seated position with your head and neck supported.
- ✦ Access peripheral vision. This is the expanded awareness you relax into when driving a familiar route, where you're looking ahead but can see out of the corners of your eyes.
- ✦ After a few moments, gently close your eyes. If you can, maintain the expanded awareness of peripheral vision.
- ✦ Loosen and soften your jaw.
- ✦ Relax the back of your tongue and allow it to settle gently into your lower jaw.
- ✦ Pay attention to your breathing. Don't try to change it, but lightly hold the expectation that it will gradually slow down.
- ✦ Bring to mind the change you wish to make, the question to which you would like answers, the personal quality you most wish to cultivate, and wait in an attitude of gratitude. Trust that the deepest, wisest part of you is listening, and will assist in every way.

If you already have a meditation practice in place, this will be an easy adjustment, a chance to experiment with some new approaches drawn from the field of hypnotherapy. But if you're new to this, then begin with a few minutes at a time at first, extending out eventually to ten minutes or longer. Whatever you can manage is better than nothing, so don't let the perfect be the enemy of the good. Consistency is more important than duration, so carve out a few minutes a day at first until you begin to reap the benefits and find you have time for more.

You may find that a little instrumental music or white noise (such as rainfall or beach waves) is also helpful. And there are apps available which feature binaural beats embedded in their recordings, a gentle *thrum* underneath the sound which helps entrain your brainwaves into the optimal pattern you choose as your purpose – alpha, theta or delta.

To help you along your way, I've created a guided relaxation recording to support your effortless and authentic success. It is available to download at www.KateTrafford.com/FreeHypno. Listen regularly, and through headphones, for maximum effect. I hope you find the experience as blissful and profoundly impactful as I do.

Start and finish strong

Now that you are aware that you naturally move through trance as you wake in the morning and settle down to sleep at night, can you see the potential to start and finish strong each day? These two points in your day are ripe with far greater untapped potential than most people realise.

What do you tend to focus on when your head touches the pillow at night? Do you review the day with appreciation – celebrating your accomplishments, grateful for the support you've received, reliving and relishing the sensory pleasures, thankful for everything you've learned and gently anticipating a wonderfully restorative night's sleep? Or do you – like so many of my brilliant, hard-driving clients – rehash the day through a more fearful lens, worrying about what you didn't get done, the meaning behind that 'look' you were given, ruminating on your unsolved problems, and all the while anxious about how tired you're feeling and unwittingly mentally rehearsing getting far less sleep than you need?

And what about how you start your day? With your head on the pillow as you return to consciousness, what do you focus on then? Do you rouse gently, appreciating the warmth and comfort of your bed and gently turning your attention to the day? Do you connect to what you imagine is in store, and feel your excitement rise in anticipation of the chance to connect with your loved ones, friends and colleagues, and take inspired action towards your dreams? Or do you wake yourself harshly, resist the new start, succumb to the snooze button, until finally you can wait no longer and shout yourself out of bed like a drill sergeant?

You already know that your answers to these questions matter, since your autopilot gives you more of what you focus on, whether you want it or not. Imagine the difference it could make if you were to positively embrace the two naturally occurring trance opportunities available when your head is on your pillow. End your day strong by focusing on what you loved the most about your day and what you appreciate most in your life as a whole. Start your day in a place of appreciation for the people and other blessings in your life, and the one thing about your day you're looking forward to the most. This may not come easily at first, but your autopilot will soon pick up the request. And because you took the small effort required to focus on these two points, the power of trance will amplify the effect. Author and wellbeing teacher Louise Hay said it best in her book *Heal Your Body A-Z* (2004):

'How you start your day is how you live your day. How you live your day is how you live your life.'

Now you have your missing owner's manual for your incredible mind–body vehicle, it's time to commit with joy to the next stage of your authentic adventure. Let's plot a course to your dream destination, one that allows you to make a difference for others by bringing your best self to the moment. Let's look beyond the traditional approaches to action planning and productivity – which are often of limited value in a fast-paced and rapidly changing environment – and explore the practical and pragmatic approaches that will help you get traction and build momentum.

It's time to think like an intrepid explorer and make progress like a pro.

PART FOUR
Thrive As You Drive

14. Think Like an Intrepid Explorer

The real voyage of discovery consists not in seeking new landscapes, but in having new eyes.

– Marcel Proust, *La Prisonnière* (1923)
French novelist, critic and essayist

Strengthen your strategy

I can still remember as a child in primary school hearing the story of the 1911 race to the South Pole. To my wide-eyed ten-year-old self, the extraordinary tale of rival teams led by Antarctic explorers Robert Falcon Scott and Roald Amundsen was the most nail-biting adventure I'd ever heard told. And I wasn't the only one who was enthralled. The story was relayed by our teacher in stages, with each day's lesson ending on an abrupt cliffhanger that triggered a collective groan from the entire class. We couldn't wait to hear what happened next.

If you know the story, then you'll know it didn't end well for the British team. They were beaten to the Pole by their Norwegian counterparts, who'd arrived a full 34 days earlier. Our lessons were an analysis of the British team's many *failures* – taking ponies instead of dogs, relying on mechanical sledges without including the engineer in their team, and spacing their food and fuel depots too far apart.

Scott and most of his team perished on the return leg of their journey. There wasn't a dry eye in the classroom as our teacher told the poignant story of Captain Oates, who sacrificed himself in hopes of saving his fellow travellers, uttering the immortal last words (recorded in Scott's diary), 'I am just going outside and may be some time.'

Whether it was what our teacher *actually* shared in those lessons, or simply the selective filtering of my ten-year-old brain, I can't say for sure. What I can say is that it would be many years before it would even occur to me to look past the question 'Why did Scott fail?', and instead ask the far more important question: 'How did Amundsen *succeed*?'

The answer, I've since discovered, came down to strategy. Given the huge uncertainties he faced, Amundsen knew that traditional approaches to planning and preparation simply wouldn't cut it. Much of the knowledge of how to survive and navigate in regions of extreme cold either didn't exist or was held by groups outside his own community of elite explorers. For this reason, he spent significant amounts of time living with and learning from the Inuit people of northern Canada. He conducted numerous experiments and mini-expeditions to discover what he and his team would need to know. And he worked tirelessly to piece together the elements of an overall strategy and tactical plan that would see himself and all 19 of his team members achieve their extraordinary goal and return safe and well. What worked was Amundsen's willingness to *embrace uncertainty*, and to have his inner protector and inner adventurer work hand in hand.

So what was Amundsen's world-beating strategy for intrepid exploration? Here are the key enablers of his incredible accomplishment:

- breaking his journey into stages, and marking the way with milestones he could focus on, move towards and celebrate reaching
- making sure he had the right people on his team, including the best possible guides
- running scenarios of various potential outcomes and taking aligned action in advance, ensuring that his journey would continue robustly *no matter which scenario unfolded*
- building redundancy into his supplies, knowing he'd be adequately resourced even in his worst-case scenario
- testing and piloting his ideas by running a series of mini-expeditions, learning from both what did and did not work, and feeding this learning forward into his next experiment or attempt
- expecting to go 'off course' at times and building in tracking systems and metrics to help him recognise the detours so he could readily course-correct
- putting tools and systems in place to support his success, so he didn't have to do all the heavy lifting himself
- shifting cleanly and frequently between navigating and driving on, ensuring he fulfilled both roles superbly well
- staying present to reality however his journey unfolded, pausing when the conditions were not conducive to progress but committing to make progress whenever possible
- dedicating himself to a lifelong journey of personal mastery – evolving his mindset, 'heartset' and skillset in pursuit of his dream destination.

Now if that strategy worked for a never-been-done-before intrepid adventure in the most hostile territory on Earth, think what it could do for you.

So how will you reach your dream destination and

eventually your ultimate dream? As your journey unfolds, how will you know you're on the right track? It's time to plot a course and mark your map with some magical milestones.

Mark your magical milestones

Focusing toward a big dream can be daunting. Our ever-changing world can make it challenging to plot a course, even in outline. It's not easy to plan ahead if it seems like the plan will be out of date before the ink has even dried.

To see your journey clearly, you must rise above it all. From a higher vantage point you can see at least your major milestones – albeit separated by broad areas of uncharted territory.

By breaking your journey down into stages, you'll soon identify your magical milestones – the intermediate arrival points that carry the essential thrill of your dream destination – and perhaps your ultimate dream, the work of a lifetime. These magical milestones are way-markers that let you know you're on the right track, following your most authentic path. They are the accomplishments that mark your growth and contribution along the way, and that encourage you to celebrate progress, to feel like you are *always arriving*.

And even if your ultimate dream does feel like the work of a lifetime, each magical milestone simply becomes a three-to-five-year dream destination in its own right, each with its own magical milestones. For example, en route to my own ultimate dream, I knew writing and sharing this book would be a magical milestone. But it felt like a significant dream in its own right, so I set 'published author' as a specific dream destination. I had no idea how to move forward at first, but I knew at least some of the magical milestones I'd celebrate along the way – signing with a publisher, first full draft manuscript, choosing a front cover design, and so on. The joy of this approach is that it brings even your most magnificent vision for this lifetime into the here-and-now, allowing you to tap into the thrill power inspired by your ultimate dream.

Here's the top tip that makes identifying your magical milestones *much easier*:

Stop trying to plan ahead from where you are now. Instead, imagine you have already reached your dream destination, and trace your journey backwards from there.

By tapping into the vantage point of your authentic future self, you'll be able to work back from your accomplishment identifying the intermediate stages you navigated. Remember to *envision* your journey: don't try to figure this out with your conscious mind alone. Immerse yourself in your dream destination first, and explore what you are shown.

For example, if you know where you want to be three years from now, ask yourself, 'What's true at the two-year milestone?' Get curious and let your future self show you how it all came about. Once you have a strong sense of that, including a few of the specifics that will surprise and delight you, it's time to pull back to the one-year mark. And then back to six months.

Don't just plan for your vision – envision your plan

A couple of crucial points of guidance if you want to make this approach work for you. First, there is a way you can tell if you've truly *envisioned* your magical milestones, or if your well-intentioned but over-zealous conscious mind has grasped the wheel. Your conscious mind will have a tendency to intellectualise this process, and in so doing, split a three-year accomplishment fairly evenly across three one-year stages. It says, 'Well, if you want to achieve that by Year 2, then you must've achieved this by the end of Year 1.' But that's rarely the way authentic success unfolds. You'll know you've *envisioned* success when you see that the progress you've plotted across the years is not a straight line, but a 'hockey stick' curve (see Fig. 14.1).

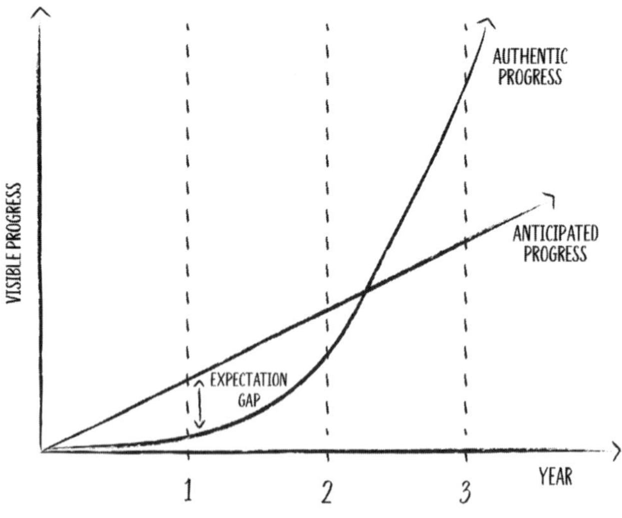

Fig. 14.1: 'Hockey Stick' Curve of Authentic Success

Tangible outputs tend to be modest at first, as you focus on laying the groundwork, making connections with others who can help you, running mini-expeditions to test and check and discover exactly what you need to know to reach your dream destination. Without this awareness, it's easy to overestimate what can be achieved in Year 1, and this expectation gap can lead to disappointment and demotivation. But once the magic of momentum kicks in – due to your ever-increasing clarity, focus, skill and connections – the rate of progress begins to rapidly increase, which means we often underestimate what can be joyfully achieved in two years, three years or more. That's how you'll know you've truly engaged with your authentic future self. While your dream destination may feel stretching – perhaps even awe inspiring – your earliest magical milestones will seem very accessible, with plenty of time built in for research and reconnaissance.

The second point to bear in mind is how easy it can be to get attached to time frames in a way that does not serve you. It can be inspiring to bring your whole self to a goal with soul, and thrilling to lean in with the curiosity of an intrepid explorer, knowing where you'd like to get to but not precisely how you'll get there. But if the deadline starts to trigger you into fear, you'll soon slip back into driving hard and rob yourself of the joy of the journey. What's more, your attachment to the plan, rather than to the magical milestone itself, may mean you drive on by when circumstances shift and miss an inspired shortcut. Remember, if you listen to your inner satnav, there'll be no end of guidance offered along the way. Your journey may take longer than you first imagined, and if you're driving happy, who cares? This is an adventure, not a relentless race. Conversely, I've lost count of the number of times I've worked with a client on a five-year plan, only to have them come back to me two or three years later and say, 'I'm almost there. Can we re-set?'

Let your magical milestones inspire you to ask the right questions, challenge any assumed limitations and commit to spending at least a little time each day in the courage zone. Whether you've already got momentum and you're excited for more, or you're embarking on your authentic adventure from a standing start, progress is always possible. You can get there *and* love here.

Find your guide

Your dream destination – and the adventure it inspires – are uniquely yours. But at every stage there will be individuals who have charted at least some aspects of your terrain – those who can show you the way, and relish their own journeys even more as a result.

Take another look at the life of anyone you deeply admire and you'll find a second factor that they all have in common: the greatness they achieved, including the greatness they realised within themselves, was a *team* effort. They had teachers, mentors, companions and guides, and they allowed that convoy of co-creators to evolve over time as they did.

So, who do you want and need in *your* convoy? Of course, you may have several spots already reserved for your loved ones, those who help bring meaning to your authentic endeavours. Beyond that, who will be your travelling companions? Who will help you find your way? And how can you tap into the collective wisdom of mastermind groups, professional institutions and personal development groups, so that you can grow as you go? Let's begin by considering how you can find your initial guide – the Obi-Wan Kenobi to your Luke Skywalker – the mentor who can guide and support you as you first cross from familiar to unfamiliar territory.

When seeking a guide, there's no need to leave the matching process to chance. You don't have to wait for your company to assign you to a mentor. You can shift into your courage zone and respectfully approach the person you most admire, the individual whose unique vantage point on work and life might clarify and enrich your own mental map.

When seeking a mentor, remember not to focus on achievement alone: connect with someone who can both speak to the nature of the terrain you're intending to travel and support you in *travelling well.*

Be mindful of unconscious bias, and even conscious vested interests. It's essential that you approach someone you believe will strive to be impartial in the guidance they offer. These conversations are not purely about your performance in your current role. They are about you and your medium- to long-term career aspirations. For this reason, no matter how brilliant your boss may be, it's usually wise to find a mentor who is not in your immediate line of management. An impartial mentor who has little or no vested interest in the choices you make can be an invaluable sounding board, particularly as you approach any significant career crossroads, such as whether to stay in your current role or move on to something new. And if it's too much to ask that your mentor be completely impartial, then at least be sure to draw on multiple perspectives before coming to your own conclusions.

Who comes to mind now as a potential mentor, someone:

- ✦ you admire
- ✦ who's further down the road you intend to travel
- ✦ and who you believe best fits the criteria outlined above?

If you are not already connected, do you have a connection in common who might be willing to introduce you? What would be your best first step in approaching them to ask for help and guidance?

Create a two-way street

If you're hesitating at this point, believing that your request is too much to ask, bear in mind that the most valuable mentoring relationships are a two-way street. This process will be invaluable to you, but your insights, talents and energy are potentially invaluable to them too. Mentoring relationships that feel reciprocal are more likely to last for the long haul – if that's what you *both* want. So, consider how you can contribute to this person and add value to their work and life. What perspective can you offer to them that could enrich their own map? How might you ensure that they look forward to their time with you as one of the high points of their schedule, something that rarely if ever gets bumped in favour of something seemingly more pressing?

While it is, of course, appropriate to be deeply respectful towards anyone generous enough to share their time and insights, don't let awe tip you over into excessive deference. Yes, they are further down the road than you in some respects, but you are both whole human beings, and you are also worthy of respect. Ensure confidentiality is in place, so that you can both be confident what's said in the room stays in the room.

Remember that you are looking for *input only* – thought-provoking questions, ideas and experience from another perspective – *not* for someone to tell you what to do. When the way ahead is unclear, the idea of having someone who can tell you exactly what you need to do may be comforting. But blindly following the guidance of anyone else, no matter how much of an authority you consider them to be, is a high-risk strategy. There are few absolute rights and wrongs, and *only you can decide* what's right for you and wrong for you. Listen to your mentor, but listen to your inner satnav too!

Go out to others for data, but come back home to yourself for decisions.

If you want to go far...

Finding a mentor is only one way to draw on the wisdom of others. Authentic success – driving happy, not hard – can be a team effort. Be open to connecting with a wider network of individuals who can challenge and facilitate your thinking, encourage you and perhaps illuminate just one or two key aspects of your journey. There will be helpers, companions and guides who can support you on your authentic adventure, and you can take great pleasure in helping them in return. This leads to success that lasts for the long haul. As the saying goes,

'If you want to go fast, go alone;
If you want to go far, go together.'

Here are some further opportunities to grow your convoy of fellow travellers, so you can make swift, sustainable and enjoyable progress together.

Take a look through the following list, and consider which of the following feel most inspiring and energising to you. Choose just one for now, and make one small move to get started.

- **Masterminding** – Connect with a small number of peers to offer one another challenge and support, and encourage each other's progress. This may be peers within your own company or industry, or an eclectic mix of highly capable and aspirational professionals with whom you just click. Meet regularly, share the airtime evenly, and be supportive and solution oriented in your approach.
- **Professional networking** – Professional bodies established in support of your sector, industry or technical profession can be a great source of ideas, market intelligence and opportunities for continuing professional development. They can also help you meet the right people and make the connections you need in support of your long-term aspirations. Offering to get involved in running a local or regional group can also give

you a chance to develop your leadership skills, give you VIP access to expert guest speakers and help raise your profile and strengthen your personal brand.

- **Personal development groups** – If you want to grow as you go, find a group outside work that provides a safe space in which to stretch yourself, and develop the mindset, heartset and skillset you need for your authentic adventure. Many personal development organisations offer a community space for those who attend their programmes, or you can find out what's open to anyone and already available in your area or online using sites such as MeetUp and Eventbrite.

Remember not to become overly focused on just the information you can pick up or the skills you can develop.

You will be shaped by the beliefs, values and attitudes of the people you spend the most time with. So, when you attend your first meeting or two, ask yourself, 'Do I want to be *more like these people*?' If the answer is 'no', keep looking.

Now you have your dream destination in mind and your zone of genius in play. You have a strategy and a map marked with magical milestones. And you have a convoy of wonderful people around you, ready to move forward on purpose. It's time to make your move.

15. Make Progress Like a Pro

Do something today your future self will thank you for.

– attributed to Sean Patrick Flanery
Actor, author and martial artist

Bump starting from stalled

I well remember when I first understood the significance of 'inertia'. Not the meaning of the word – at around eight years old I was a little too young for that. But I was certainly old enough to understand – and be fascinated by – the experience of it.

You see, our family had a car that occasionally just wouldn't start. A few turns of the engine with no response, and we all knew what came next. My dad would shout, 'Everybody out!' and my two sisters, my nan and I would pile out of the car and around to the back. What a sight we must have made for the neighbours, lined up from age six to 60-plus, all leaning in with gusto trying to get this mass of metal moving.

Getting started was always the hardest part, so Dad would help in the beginning, pushing with one hand on the door sill and the other on the steering wheel. Then, as soon as we were rolling, he'd leap into the driver's seat, make his move, and the engine would burst into life. We all ran after him, cheering and giggling until he pulled to a halt, revving the engine a little just to be sure. 'Couldn't have done it without you, girls!' Dad would declare, and we'd clamber back into the car, beaming with pride at our brilliant achievement and the teamwork that got us there.

Now let's acknowledge that, from time to time, *you* too may need to mobilise from a standing start. That might be because you're embarking on a new phase of your journey – a new project, a new role, or life in a new location – which can be incredibly exciting but also overwhelming at first. Or it might be because you're reeling from a recent setback that's left you feeling stalled. Either way, getting started from a standstill always involves overcoming some initial inertia.

So how can you bump-start your productivity when you're overanalysing, overcommitted or overwhelmed? The good news is it can be a lot easier, and a lot more enjoyable, than you might have experienced in the past.

Release the brakes

The effort required to take action from a standing start is known in psychology as 'activation energy'. This required effort can range from a barely perceptible dip into your willpower to a sizeable struggle, depending on factors both inside and outside yourself. Internal *resistance* is like driving with the handbrake still on. It can grind you to a halt, or even stop you from getting started in the first place. And even if you do make progress, all that unaddressed resistance takes its toll on your 'vehicle'. Outside yourself is the *drag*, the environmental friction that results from misaligned relationships and inefficient systems. If you want to maximise your momentum and make progress like a pro, it's time to optimise both.

Let's begin by releasing the brakes. To do this, recognise that you are freedom-seeking by nature, and your deep, soul-level self knows you to be free to choose what you do, when and with whom. That means that when you say to yourself, 'I've *got to* do this' or 'I've got *no choice*', you create unnecessary internal resistance: your satnav will let you know your thinking is off, and the resistance you feel makes it harder than necessary to take the required action.

The reality is you always have a choice about what you do and don't do: you just might not like the natural consequences of *choosing inaction*. Not showing up for work when expected may cost you your job. Not paying your bills may cost you your home and its services. Not submitting your tax return on time may cost you a fine. Not visiting your dentist may cost you your teeth. But you do still have a *choice*.

So, the next time you have something to do that you perceive *must* be done, avoid making it harder than it needs to be. Recognise that you do have a choice, and all things considered you are more aligned with choosing action than inaction.

Release your resistance by telling yourself the truth: '*I choose this now.*'

Next, remember that you can always ask for help – practical assistance, advice or even a little moral support as you courageously cross into unfamiliar territory. Lean into your friends, colleagues and extended family for support. Even if you don't know anyone who can help with your particular challenge, the chances are you know someone who does.

A final note on overcoming procrastination. Understand

that it is not the task itself you're bouncing off, but *the way the task makes you feel*. If you're confused or unsure, or the scrutiny and stakes seem high, this will trigger a fear-based response that means you're much more likely to avoid the task and do something else instead. This is why when you approach the writing of an important report, bid, academic paper or presentation you may find yourself inexplicably clearing out a cupboard instead.

Procrastination ends the moment the focus of your fear shifts, and the pain of the potential consequences of not completing the task becomes greater than the pain anticipated in completing it.

That's why the tipping point from inaction to action can be so sudden, and lead to an adrenaline-fuelled frenzy of activity that could have been completed to a significantly higher standard – and far more calmly and enjoyably – if only you'd started sooner.

Get ready to make your move

Is there an important task that's been on your To Do list for far too long? If so, it's time to release the brakes. Do this by recognising that it's not the task itself you're avoiding but the uncomfortable feelings that arise as you imagine completing the task.

- Take up your travel journal and ask yourself, 'How does the idea of tackling this task make me feel?' Anxious? Incompetent? Guilty? Bored? Whatever your answer, recognise that it is *not the task itself* that feels that way, but *the thoughts you are thinking* about the task. So now you can play the 'Warmer, warmer' game, and *feel* your way into a more aligned perspective:
- Tune into how good you'll feel when the task is completed.
- Focus on developing a particular skill or acquiring knowledge along the way that will serve you on your authentic adventure.
- Find ways to gamify your progress, to catch yourself being brilliant and make it more fun.

Focus on the process of the task, instead of the high-stakes outcome, and get the job done one small, inspired move at a time.

Even if you are already at full capacity in your existing roles and responsibilities – both at work and at home – commit to making at least one small move each day in the direction of your dreams. If you consistently take even the tiniest of inspired actions, the authentic energy you will unleash will surprise and delight you. And that authentic inspiration will begin to trickle through everything that 'must be done'. You'll soon be inspired towards more effective and efficient ways of doing what's *necessary*, creating more space for what's *possible*.

I encourage you to keep a record of these authentic achievements, no matter how big or how small, momentarily parking your to-do list to build up a '*Ta-da!*' list. By noting and celebrating the inspired moves you make in the direction of your dreams – *Ta-da!* – you'll catch yourself being brilliant, reinforcing your authentic self-confidence, and creating a feel-good feed-forward loop that helps you build and maintain your momentum. Consistency matters more than the scale of each move. So take the advice offered in the brilliant opening quote of this chapter: 'Do *something* today that your future self will thank you for.'

Trigger your true choices

Now you know how to overcome inertia when mobilising from a standing start or even when switching from one task to another. So how can you use the idea of 'activation energy' to help you make authentic choices even when your autopilot programming isn't yet quite up to speed? The answer lies in recognising the environmental triggers that drive these choices, and change them so that activation energy works *for* you rather than against you. That means:

- *decreasing* the activation energy required for behaviours you *want* to do (making them easier to start)
- *increasing* the activation energy required for behaviours that you *don't want* to do (making them harder to start).

Let's begin by thinking about a healthy new habit, such as starting your day with a walk or a run. Until your amazing autopilot takes over and turns the task into a habit, every tiny choice point will be navigated consciously. Each small decision takes a little bit of willpower which, as we explored in Chapter 3, is a finite resource. Reducing the activation energy required to engage in your morning exercise might mean taking a few simple planning and navigation actions the night before:

- laying out your exercise clothes (or, as one coaching client did at first, even sleeping in them!)
- putting together an uplifting and energising playlist
- deciding the route you will take
- placing your training shoes by the front door
- arranging to meet a friend – either virtually or in real life – so you've got the pleasure of their company *and* help in holding yourself accountable, meaning you're also less likely to ditch the idea while still cosy under your quilt.

And that final point leads us to the other side of the equation. How can you *make it harder to do the old, automatic behaviour*? You might:

- put your alarm clock on the opposite side of the room
- buy a cheaper train or bus ticket to work, so you have to get off a stop early and walk the rest of the way
- commit to raising funds for a favourite charity.

Anything that triggers your authentic choice and makes it harder to follow the established or easy options counts.

As well as using this approach to reinforce specific new habits, you can apply the same principles more generally to help you stay on track with your authentic adventure. For example, I recommend switching off notifications on your computer and smartphone so that you are not constantly distracted away by other people's priorities. You can still designate certain key contacts – loved ones, key colleagues, your children's school, etc. – as 'VIPs' so notifications from them still come through, but it's crucial to cut down on distractions as best you can. And that means also being honest with yourself about the amount of time you spend aimlessly surfing and scrolling.

Remember that some of the best brains in Silicon Valley are paid a small fortune to hook you into social media, entertainment and news sites, and to keep you there for as long as possible.

Their compelling colour schemes and endless 'recommendation' loops based on your own past browsing or the interests of your friends make it far easier to continue to scroll than to break out once you're in.

If scrolling is an autopilot habit that triggers every time you're bored or overwhelmed, consider removing the apps from your smartphone altogether or downloading a management app that allows you to set limits on when you can access these sites and for how long.

Finally, one simple solution for membership sites is to remove the automatic login feature, meaning you have to enter your username and password every time. The few seconds it takes to do this may be all the activation energy required to break you out of the trance of your old autopilot programme, giving you cause to pause and make a fresh conscious choice.

Navigating uncertainty

As your authentic adventure unfolds, there may well be points in your journey where you *want* to take inspired action, but you're simply not sure what to do for the best. We've already explored how you can dissolve your dilemmas and make a truly authentic choice when the time comes. But there may also be situations where there's a great deal of uncertainty, and where you don't yet have enough information to commit to a particular course of action.

When the road has yet to unfold, playing the situation out in your mind too far into the future can be stressful, as your inner protector grasps for data that's simply not yet available. In such situations, it can appear as though there is nothing more you *can* do until more information comes in. And if the factors that will generate that new information are outside your control – decisions that will be made by others, shifts in the economy, etc. – this can lead to a feeling of powerlessness or frustration as you spin your wheels waiting for some kind of sign.

The answer is found once again in Amundsen's strategy:

Identify the small number of *scenarios* that *might* unfold and consider, in broad terms, *the best way forward for each.*

When you do this, you'll clearly see that there are inspired actions you can take *right now* that will serve you no matter which scenario plays out.

As an example of how profound the impact of this scenario-planning approach can be, I'll share an experience that unfolded in the first few weeks of the 2020 COVID pandemic. I received an urgent message from a past client, a brilliant emerging leader I'd worked with as part of his company's talent development programme. I was shocked to hear that, along with hundreds of others at his grade in the company, he'd been put on a 90-day notice of being at risk of redundancy. From the moment our call began, the barriers of belief came tumbling out. 'Who's going to be hiring in this economy?' he asked, clearly not expecting a reply. 'I've got a mortgage to pay.' And within the first few minutes, it became clear that he felt paralysed by one particularly significant barrier of belief: how his career played out from here would be decided by others in a room he wouldn't be in, based on a conversation he felt powerless to influence, and 'anywhere up to 90 days from now'.

I began by acknowledging that there was, indeed, a great deal of uncertainty in his situation and that it was true that some of the information he might need would come from others on a time frame he could not influence. However, I pointed out that he could find some certainty right now by getting clear on the *process* he could follow to get the information he needed. Even more importantly, he could *remain certain within himself* that he had a great deal to offer to his future employer, whether he stayed where he was or moved on elsewhere, and that he could leverage his strengths and talents to navigate this challenging terrain one small, inspired move at a time.

By identifying the main scenarios for how his journey might unfold and exploring and optimising his best way forward in each scenario, he visibly relaxed and eventually became quite animated as new possibilities emerged. I encouraged him to embrace the upside of uncertainty:

**When nothing is certain,
anything is possible.**

The final step was to sift all the potential inspired actions that had emerged and identify those which would serve him *no matter which scenario played out*. These actions clustered around him getting clearer than ever on:

- ✦ what he was uniquely positioned to contribute in any future role
- ✦ which aspects of his work he most enjoyed
- ✦ his long-term career aspirations
- ✦ how best to showcase his offer in his personal marketing materials (CV, *LinkedIn* profile, etc.) so that *no matter what happened next* he was good to go.

'Wow!' he beamed. 'I've got a lot to do. And I can't wait to get started!'

Embracing uncertainty

In situations like the example above, it's important to acknowledge that the risks you perceive when you hit a roadblock – be it an unexpected setback or a tantalising but stretching opportunity – have not gone away. My client was right to note that he had a mortgage to pay and to focus on securing his income. Your risks do need to be identified, managed and mitigated. So, if you're navigating uncertainty, identify those inspired actions that make the most sense to prioritise right now.

With practice, you can go beyond just tolerating uncertainty and learn to actively embrace it. When you trust yourself to handle the journey, however it unfolds, uncertainty becomes your ally – the source of an endless stream of new possibilities and opportunities. You can navigate the most challenging terrain, and still feel like the right person in the right place at the right time.

Now you're thinking like an intrepid explorer and making progress like a pro, how can you maximise your momentum? It's time to see how you can rework your systems so they really work for you.

16. The Magic of Momentum

Realise that you'll never get everything done. That's not the game any more. Be safe in the knowledge that you're in control, selecting the right things to do, and that you're doing as much as one human being possibly can.

– Graham Allcott, *How to Be a Productivity Ninja* (2015)
British author and speaker on productivity and leadership

Soup up your systems

It's not just driving with the brakes on that slows you down. That internal resistance can be made significantly worse by resistance on the outside – the drag of misaligned systems and surroundings. So, if you want to maximise your momentum and make progress like a pro, begin by reviewing and reworking the systems you use to support your productivity.

Having simple, elegant, fit-for-purpose systems in place is as close as you can currently get to cloning yourself! It's also an area you can tackle progressively over time, and one where small changes can make a big difference.

Throughout the book so far, we've covered ideas that can help you get traction and build your momentum, and these strategies can be applied in many different ways to help you achieve greater ease and flow. Let's briefly review them now, and add in a few bonus productivity tips:

- **Monthly planning.** This is the big picture approach that allows you to set priorities that align with your 'magical milestones'. Recognising that your capacity to deliver against both personal and professional projects is limited, you'll make far greater progress overall if you focus primarily on just two or three significant projects at a time. What are your authentic priorities for the month ahead?
- **Weekly planning.** This is by far the most powerful time frame for productive planning, as it allows you to bridge the planning gap, and ensure you are making healthy progress towards your magical milestones, prioritising what is most *important* to you rather than the merely *urgent*. You may wish to keep your work and personal planning separate, but many of my clients have found that an integrated approach at the weekly planning stage is most effective as you're more likely to take care of yourself and your loved ones as well as taking care of business. What do you most want to achieve in the week ahead? How might this differ from what is expected, meaning you may need to have courageous conversations with others? What can you learn from what went well last week and what could have been even better?
- **Daily planning.** This is where you zoom in and set your intentions for the day and prioritise the real challenges and opportunities coming your way. You may find this is best done at the end of the day before, when you can determine one to three priorities for the *next* day and commit to clearing these. This will help you navigate healthy boundaries more effectively when urgent (but not necessarily as *important*) requests come in.

- **Habit stacking.** This entails tying two activities together so they take no extra time, and you're more likely to remember to do both, such as when I suggested you envision your dream destination a couple of times a day while brushing your teeth or exercising with a friend. What else could you link together so you can effortlessly prioritise more of what matters most?

Make space for meaningful progress

If you truly want to prioritise what's truly important – the activities that have the potential to make the biggest difference to you and the people around you – then there's another roadblock that must be overcome: the endless stream of distractions and demands. Yes, there are certain activities that simply must be taken care of, both personally and professionally. But often, prioritising what matters to others over what matters most to you is nothing more than habit. And when we add the tempting distractions of news, entertainment and social media sites, it's a wonder anything meaningful gets done. Even when you keep your focus on your work, it's easy to mistake busyness for progress, especially when you're stressed, tired or overwhelmed.

Here are some bonus suggestions to take you beyond simply getting more done, helping you to make space for truly meaningful progress:

- **Time blocking.** This is setting aside larger chunks of time for an uninterrupted deep dive into a single major task or by clustering similar activities together, which minimises time lost through switching from task to task. How could you use time blocking for greater efficiency and focus when you have creative work or even a batch of admin to handle? How can you match the timing of these blocks to the natural fluctuations in your focus and energy levels through the day? And what boundaries might you need to agree with colleagues and even family around your availability?

- **Co-working.** Whether virtual or in person, silent working with others can create a safe and supportive environment for focused productivity. Where, when and with whom could you co-work? And how could you make it a regular practice, so your autopilot makes it progressively easier and easier? (More on making co-working work for you in just a moment.)
- **Silence notifications.** Generally, but even more importantly when time blocking, minimise interruptions from your smartphone by going into airplane mode or by using a more selective notification management app. Notifications cost you dearly, not only because of the time each interruption costs you, but also because they programme your autopilot to take you to the phone/web like one of Pavlov's salivating dogs. How can you make it easier for yourself to stay focused? Who do you need to add as VIP exceptions to your notification blackout (e.g. one or two key clients or colleagues, or emergency calls from your child's school)?
- **Email management.** Resist the urge to constantly check your emails. Tackle your inbox at regular intervals throughout the day. You may wish to manage others' expectations by including this in your email signature, along with a prompt for how you can be reached if the message is truly urgent.
- **Prioritise systemic improvements.** If there are systems, processes and workflows that you use frequently, prioritise improvements and upgrades that will save

you time, energy or frustration. When you strip out the struggle, you can redirect the time and energy saved into other areas, meaning you are building your effectiveness, not just your efficiency.

Connect with your co-working convoy

Once you have souped up your systems and your planning, workflows and email management are ticking over nicely, how can you enjoy making progress and build your momentum still further? The key is in remembering that...

Even when there's work that *only you* can do, you don't have to do it alone.

By far my biggest productivity discovery of 2020 was the power of virtual co-working: jumping on to a video call with one or more friends and colleagues, and making quiet progress together. In fact, most of the book you now hold in your hands was written in early morning writing sessions with my 'book buddies' – a small group of aspiring authors who supported one another through the ups and downs of the creative journey.

This virtual co-working strategy was originally a response to the first coronavirus lockdown, but now it's built into my success strategies for the long haul. In addition to my early morning writing/creativity sessions, I co-work for a two-hour block, at least twice weekly, and use the time for anything ranging from routine admin to deep creative work. It's not easy to explain the boost that comes from virtual co-working, but feedback from the participants in the 'co-working convoy' I host suggests it's a combination of factors:

- shared accountability (you stay in your seat)
- psychological safety (you feel supported, even in silence)

- intention setting (you say upfront what you'll tackle and at the end how much progress you made)
- conditioned productivity (the more you do it, and enjoy success, the more your autopilot primes you to make progress).

Ready to give virtual co-working a whirl?

- Decide who you'd like to work with and share the idea.
- Set aside a block of time and arrange to meet.
- Commit to silent working for at least 50 minutes in each one-hour period so that everyone can come along confident progress will be made.
- Take the first few minutes of each hour to check in with one another, and to set your intentions for the time ahead (in larger co-working groups, this intention-setting can be done in the chat box).
- Take the last few minutes of the hour to check in again and celebrate progress.
- You can also quickly troubleshoot any glitches if someone in the group is struggling, but avoid extended discussions.
- Fifty minutes of productive focus per hour is the minimum commitment, so be sure to schedule follow-up discussions if you're happy for more active mutual support to be part of your arrangement.

Just one more tip for making co-working work for you: remember to prioritise self-care. Co-working can create incredible momentum, and at first it can be tempting to just keep going when you're 'on a roll'. But if you meet for two hours or more, be sure to use hourly intermediate check-ins as a chance to get up and *move*. Not only is this a healthful practice, it will also refresh and reboot your mental focus. Go to the bathroom, drink plenty of water, enjoy a healthy snack – whatever your incredible mind–body vehicle needs to perform at its best.

Fast-track your feel-good

Co-working is yet another example of the power of shifting from driving hard to driving happy – from acting out of desperation to following your inspiration. And that small effort of changing your state by changing your thinking puts you in touch with effortless achievement.

Change your state first, then take action.

So how else can you change state as fast as possible? What if you find you have important work to do, but you're just 'not feeling it'? If it'll soon be your turn to step up and speak, how can you get to the courage zone in no time at all? The answer lies in creating a dedicated playlist, a brand-new soundtrack for your authentic adventure.

Music is one of the fastest and most powerful ways to change your state. It taps you straight into whatever state the composer/band/songwriter was in when the music was first made. And if it's a favourite piece from 'way back when', it'll also tap you straight back into the state you were in whenever you used to listen to it.

Most people organise their music by band, genre or even A-Z. But this misses a huge opportunity.

Create a new playlist of your all-time favourite tracks, organised by the *emotional* state they evoke.

What's the song that most energises and inspires you? My top tune is 'Happy' by Pharrell Williams. It makes me want to dance, which helps me shake off any stuck state, and the lyrics help connect my worrisome head to my fun-loving heart. This song does it for me every time.

What track belongs in that final slot of your playlist? What's the song that was the soundtrack to your youth or the highlight of the best gig you ever attended? And it doesn't matter whether it's in good taste, according to the 'music police'. In fact, if there's a cheesy tune that stops you taking yourself and your situation seriously, even better.

Now you've got your best-feeling tune, think about the other songs that take you into other states that could be useful at times.

- Just had a setback or been knocked by some harsh feedback, and your satnav is saying loud and clear, 'Turn around when possible'? What's the song that would get you into a gutsy state, in touch once again with your own personal power?

- Feeling a little overwhelmed? What track helps you find a peaceful place of gentle gratitude?
- Want to be energised but in a flow state you can work in? What's the upbeat instrumental that allows you to focus undistracted by lyrics?

Taste in music is a personal thing, so ignore what anyone else might say or think, and pull together the music that does it for you.

Now you have the chance to create a brilliant resource you can take with you wherever you go, one that can fast-track you from feeling near powerless to being fully connected to your authentic invincibility.

Reorder your playlist so that it starts with the lowest state (e.g. gutsy, angry, rebellious) and ends with your top tune (excited, blissed out, invincible). Then sequence all your favourite songs by the *emotional state* they evoke in you. Bridge the gap between despair and bliss with songs/instrumentals that make you feel resilient, hopeful, optimistic, enthusiastic and passionate.

When you want to change states quickly, simply notice how you're feeling, choose the next song/state up from there and plug yourself in. You'll soon find you don't need to listen to the whole song: a few bars might be all it takes to put you in the vicinity of the next state along, and you can skip forward as soon as you're ready. You can go from the ditch of despair to feeling like an unstoppable force of nature in a matter of minutes.

So, the next time you hit a roadblock, before you do anything else, change your state. You'll be amazed that the issue that looked like an unwelcome disturbance from your comfort zone, or a major crisis from the chaos zone, when viewed from the courage zone looks like a challenge ripe with opportunity. And from that state, anything's possible.

Maximise your momentum

One final practical tip to help you overcome and avoid procrastination and maximise your momentum: make good use of 'the five-second rule', first shared by Mel Robbins in her 2011 TEDx talk (see Resources section at the end of this book for a link).

The idea is simple. When the impulse arises to take action, move within five seconds. Five seconds is the sweet spot period of time to encourage authentic, aligned action. It is long enough to pause and connect to your most authentic choice, meaning you avoid being instantaneously taken off track by bouncing off an uncomfortable feeling, but it is not so long that you hesitate, overthink and allow your fearful inner protector to apply the brakes.

To use the five-second rule, when an impulse arises to take action, immediately begin a mental countdown from five to one and make some kind of move before the countdown expires. If the inspired action is small, this is all it takes. If the inspired idea is a big one, simply move your body and orientate yourself to your first small step.

The five-second rule can help you to:

- lean in when an exciting opportunity arises in a meeting
- make the important call you've been putting off
- ask for help when you need it
- hit send on the email that's been sitting in your drafts folder
- follow a healthy impulse towards self-care if you find yourself in front of the fridge when you're not really hungry or about to toss your training shoes to the back of the cupboard
- rouse up in the morning with plenty of time to start your day strong, resisting the siren call of the snooze button.

When you give yourself just enough time to connect to who you really are and your most aligned choice, but not enough time to overthink and talk yourself out of acting on that choice, you'll be amazed by the energy you will unleash and the momentum you can create. For a full exploration of how you can apply this powerful approach, both personally and professionally, see Mel Robbins' excellent book, *The 5 Second Rule* (2017), and make procrastination a thing of the past.

And that is how you make progress like a pro. Align your systems, your state and your choices with who you most want to be, what you most want to do and contribute, and harness the magic of momentum. Others will look at you and wonder how you manage to get so much done and still enjoy vibrant good health, rich relationships and an endless stream of inspired ideas. And you can tell them.

Discover who you really are.
Decide what you really want.
Do something each day your
future self will thank you for.

17. The Trip of a Lifetime

Your time is limited, so don't waste it living someone else's life. Don't be trapped by dogma, which is living with the results of other people's thinking. Don't let the noise of others' opinions drown out your own inner voice. And, most important, have the courage to follow your heart and intuition. They somehow already know what you truly want to become. Everything else is secondary.

– Steve Jobs (2005)
Co-founder of Apple Inc.

The truth about time

The above opening quote is taken from a commencement speech Steve Jobs gave to Stanford University's graduating class of 2005. The speech is just 15 minutes long but packed with insight, encouragement and wisdom. It is a deeply authentic exploration of love, loss and living life to the full, illuminated using just three stories (see Resources at the back of this book for a link to watch the speech in full).

Jobs begins with his own experience of the power of intuition, learning to follow his curiosity and trust his own loving impulses, even when they clashed with the desires and expectations of others. He follows with lessons learned from his own perceived failures, including his very public ousting from the board of what was then Apple Computer, Inc., concluding that nothing is ever really going wrong – even when it seems undeniable that it is – and that a broader perspective on life allowed him to see how everything had unfolded in support of the greatest good for all. He ends with an unflinching account of the impact of his initial diagnosis and recovery from pancreatic cancer, the disease that would eventually return and claim his life six years later. 'Your time is limited,' he says, 'so don't waste it living someone else's life.'

Steve Jobs was right. Your time *is* limited, as is mine.

But since none of us know how many days, months and years we have, this does not necessarily mean your time is scarce. It simply means it is *precious*.

In this, the final chapter of our journey together, I invite you to take the long view. Together we'll explore the energising and flow-inducing power of a lifelong journey to greatness – mastering your innate zone of genius and making your unique contribution to your family, your organisation and the world. We'll look at how you can embrace any perceived past 'failures' as essential contributors to your authentic success, repacking your 'baggage' so you can travel light. And finally, we'll consider your extraordinary potential to inspire those around you, simply by committing to inspire.

Find and follow your edge

Loving the long haul – experiencing the lifelong upward spiral of growth and contribution you were born for – is rooted in one key focus: cultivating your authentic zone of genius. As we explored in Chapter 7, this is the unique blend of natural talents, character traits and passions you bring to the world. Your experience so far has helped you develop some of these gifts into fully realised strengths and skills. And it is when you play to these innate strengths – when you bring who you really are to what's needed in the world – that you feel most fully alive. Right person, right place, right time.

In Chapter 8 you took a first run at a treasure hunt, trawling your past experiences and your aspirations for the future for clues as to your most authentic purpose. And in Chapter 9, you envisioned your dream destination, a goal with soul to inspire you forwards for the next few years or perhaps even longer.

Your journey through this book so far is just the beginning of a process that will continue to evolve as you do, if you stay connected to what matters most. Whether you have discovered your dream destination, or simply connected with a broad direction of travel, your unconscious mind now has a vision of your authentic success that will evolve as you do, unleashing the joy of your outer journey. But one thing is clear and accessible to you right now: the opportunity to engage in a lifelong *inner* journey of self-discovery and self-realisation.

Your authentic work is an outlet for self-expression. Magic happens, for you and for those around you, when you show up as who you *really* are.

Authenticity requires courage. Expressing and expanding your zone of genius involves an ongoing exploration of your own 'edge', whatever you perceive to be a limitation to your own skill, understanding or even your character. Living at your edge means repeatedly crossing the threshold between what is easy and familiar and what is challenging and unfamiliar. And every time you do so, that threshold moves out and your comfort zone expands.

A richly rewarding life's journey is the happy by-product of crossing the threshold again and again, finding and following your authentic edge.

Exploring, expressing and expanding your zone of genius is your authentic life's work. It's the gradual unwrapping of the gifts you were given at birth to be relished along the way. It is the antithesis of driving hard for short-term success. And it doesn't matter how long the journey will take. Your life's work is meant to last you a lifetime!

Expand your zone of genius

Whenever I visit London, I am always fascinated by the drivers of the iconic black cabs. While I personally know only a few routes from Euston Station to the offices of clients I most frequently visit, those cabbies have a fully joined-up mental map of Central London. This is the by-product of studying what's called *The Knowledge*. First introduced back in 1865, *The Knowledge* requires licensed drivers to memorise over 25,000 streets and 100,000 landmarks within a six-mile radius of Charing Cross – a process that requires years of riding a bike around tiny back streets plus exams and interviews to achieve and demonstrate proficiency. And this is not an end point, but rather their major magical milestone. As the landscape is reshaped by both temporary and permanent changes – new road layouts, rights of way and landmarks – the cabbie adds to their own knowledge in an ongoing and organic way that keeps them current, relevant and effective.

Likewise, excellence in your own zone of genius begins with recognising the well-worn routes with which you're already familiar, and then following your curiosity, branching out, creating new connections between previously disconnected strategies. Much of this exploration will be meaningful and compelling – a lifelong, joy-filled treasure hunt. But from time to time, the journey to excellence will require you to cross the threshold into territory you've been avoiding, perhaps because it *doesn't* come so naturally.

Map across into uncharted territory

Some years ago, a coaching client came into our session looking uncharacteristically shaken. 'I've just had some worrying news,' she began. 'One of the directors is moving on, and they want me to step up to replace him.' I was a little confused. The directorship would be a promotion and, more importantly, the role she began to describe seemed to me to meet all the authentic criteria for job satisfaction she'd discovered during our previous session. 'What's the worry?' I asked. She paused. 'I know I could do most of the job. I'd *love* to do most of it. It's essentially a people role, which is my sweet spot, and a great opportunity to influence our culture and values. It's a chance to help make this a great place to work.' She sighed, and then began nervously chewing her lip. 'The worry is that I'd also be totally responsible for the finances. I've ducked and dived, avoiding that for years. All that abstract attention to detail... it's not my thing. And if I take this role, everyone will see the gap. It'll be a disaster.'

'So, you've never been responsible for a budget?' I asked. She shook her head. 'Not even outside work?' I added, with a twinkle in my eye.

I already knew the answer. My client had previously shared her experience of a recent house move, relaying the challenges of 'flying solo' as a working single parent of two young children, and the joys of settling into their lovely new home. The transition had involved building works, dealing with a range of contractors and the management of a tight budget.

'Yes, of course, I've done it *outside* work. I'm good with money,' she replied.

'Yes, you are,' I affirmed, 'You're *great* with money. And now you're being offered the chance to apply that in work. Yes, there will be a learning curve in terms of how that translates into reading management accounts and running a sizeable profit centre, but you love to learn, don't you?'

She nodded, half-smiling as she connected one area of her mental map with another, and allowed her old limiting beliefs to begin to dissolve. 'This is the one thing that's been holding me back: the shame of feeling like I wasn't financially savvy enough to deserve a seat at the table. But now I think about it, it's really only about learning the processes and the jargon. I'm *good with money*, and I'm *a fast learner*, so I can do that.'

And one 'finance for non-financial directors' course later, she took her seat at the table.

As you consider your own dream destination, are there any gaps in your skills, strengths or mindset that you could fill with curiosity and a little joined-up thinking? Can you see the untapped potential of your zone of genius – the gifts you were given at birth, but have yet to unwrap – and how cultivating these latent talents could infuse your journey with even greater joy?

And if your dream destination, or even your emerging vision of an ultimate destination, appears to require skills, strengths or qualities that don't yet come easily to you, what existing talents, strengths and skills could you draw on to make this more enjoyable, natural and fun? What skills have you cultivated in one area of your life that could be useful in this other area? Could a personal matter be improved by treating it like a project, and applying the project management and personal effectiveness skills you've cultivated at work? Could your tenacity on the sports field be helpful in navigating the complexities at work? What personal qualities do you have that might be helpful here? What do you appreciate most about yourself when you show up as your brilliant best?

When you maintain an awareness of the wider landscape of your life, you are much more likely to spot opportunities as they arise, and to see the value of experience you have in other areas that could help you. Loving yourself for *who you've already become*, committing to sharing your gifts with the world, and meeting any perceived shortcomings with compassion and curiosity: that's the joyful way to grow as you go. As Oscar Wilde famously quipped in his 1895 play *An Ideal Husband*, 'To love oneself is the beginning of a lifelong romance.'

Repack your baggage and travel light

So, are you ready to fully appreciate yourself and celebrate who you've already become? Are you ready to embrace the life you've already lived and the choices you've made along the way as a perfect unfolding for your authentic success from here? Or does the very idea of that sound ridiculously idealistic and unbearably trite, causing you to consider tossing this book aside as future barbecue kindling?

If you want to love the long haul, that means loving your life and everyone in it, *including yourself*.

I encourage you, no I *implore* you, to look beyond any outdated programming that suggests otherwise. Shame – the feeling that you are not enough as you are, the idea that there is something about you that means you're unworthy of love and connection – is the single most toxic and debilitating state you can access. And it is a lie. As we have already explored, you were born worthy. Your worthiness does not have to be earned and does not depend on anything you can/can't do, or have/haven't done.

I'm sure you can recall decision points where you wish, with hindsight, you'd decided differently. But using hindsight in this way is torturous. It generates regret in place of insight and wisdom. Most importantly, it ignores one crucial fact: you know what you know now, not despite that experience, but *because* of it. Without these apparent setbacks, you would not be so clear on what you do and don't want in your life. Yes, there are some common threads to our fundamental human wants and needs – the means to live comfortably, nourishing relationships, time for rest and recreation – but even these desires are not universal. It is your *lived experience*, your journey so far, that has shown you what your most authentic life would look like.

You are as unique as your fingerprint, and your authentic adventure will be as unique as you are.

If there is something about you that you fear others knowing, own it, re-examine it and mine it for insights. If the issues feel big and trigger you to feel unsafe, work with a skilled helper – a therapist, counsellor or coach – who can hold a safe space for you (and if your experience includes any kind of personal trauma, ensure their practice is trauma informed). Reflect on your experience as the contrast that brought clarity, and commit to honouring yourself by living your own truth going forward so that you can bring your gifts to the world and live fully along the way. Repack your baggage, so you can travel light.

The discoveries are on the detours

A few years ago, I supported a coaching client in working through an intense and perplexing emotional reaction: her sudden and unexpected resistance to pursuing the more senior role she *thought* she'd always wanted. An opportunity had presented itself, featuring broader responsibilities, lots of stretch and potential growth, and a chance to help reshape her company's systems so they were both more efficient and more people centred. It was exactly what she'd been hoping for and diligently and joyfully working towards... until her inner protector slammed on the emergency brake. I asked her what thoughts arose when she imagined taking on the more senior role. 'I think I'm afraid I'll make a mistake,' she said. 'A really big one.'

'What if there are no mistakes?' I replied. 'What if, no matter what happens, everything is always working out for you?' Her eyebrows shot up, and then her face settled into an expression carved from stone – not-so-subtle cues she was unconvinced. I continued, 'Sometimes events unfold exactly as we hope, and other times we get a result that's different from the one we wanted and intended. Either way, if we step back far enough, we can see that *everything* that happens serves us in some way.'

I asked her to bring to mind a big 'mistake' she had made in the past. There was no need to share it with me, just bring it to mind, but she shared anyway. 'When I was 16, I sat the usual big batch of high school exams. I was bright enough that I thought I could wing it and still pass, so I did the minimum study. Instead, I spent the time having fun with my friends. I discovered boys! In the end, it was a disaster. I failed *everything*. It was so embarrassing. I had to repeat the entire year. Huge, *huge* mistake.'

I nodded. I understood. But this story was not her

highest truth. I only had to look at her to see that.

I asked her, 'Where do you think you'd be right now if you'd chosen differently?' She tilted her head in curiosity. I continued, 'If you'd chosen a different balance between your schoolwork and your social life, and passed your exams first time: where do you think you would be right now?'

'Well, I can't know for sure, but I doubt I'd be here!' she replied with a half-smile.

We explored together a range of scenarios – the likely outcome of different choices she could have made – until she recognised how profoundly and positively she was shaped by her apparent detour from success. She saw that the depth of her friendships had shaped her personality and fast-tracked her people skills. And the setback and extra year of study combined to reset her level of ambition and aspiration, inspiring her to take up a place at university. She even recognised that resit year as her first experience of project management, the beginning of a passion and skillset that had underpinned her career success to date.

As our discussion continued, my client claimed a treasure trove of personal qualities, insights and capabilities she'd cultivated during and as a direct result of her 'big mistake'. She beamed as she celebrated everything she'd discovered along the way. 'An extra 12 months in school as the catalyst for all *that*? That was time really well spent!'

We came back to the possibility that the potential 'big mistake' she had feared she might make in the new leadership role was nothing more than a scary story, that there is no such thing as failure as she had been defining it. I asked, 'If the discoveries are on the detours, are we ever really off track?'

She paused, deep in contemplation. 'No,' she replied.

'There are no mistakes, at least not in the way I used to believe. If we follow our instincts and intuition, we're always on track. And if we're learning from whatever happens – even if what happens is not what we wanted – we're still succeeding. It's weird, but I can see it so clearly now. What I thought as a kid was a big mistake, a huge setback, was actually a *shortcut*.'

She put herself forward for that bigger role.

Is there something you believe about yourself, or about your past choices, that gets in the way of you knowing your own inherent worth? If so, please look again. Your worthiness is a given. You deserve a life rich with meaning, connection and joy, not despite everything that's unfolded, but because of it.

Your past conditioning may lead you to believe that replacing your habit of shame and self-criticism with self-compassion could lead to arrogance or self-indulgence, but that's not my own or my clients' experience, and it's not what a growing body of research suggests. Feeling the lightness of being that comes when you shed excess mental and emotional weight can often play out physically too, as a step-change in self-care. It's much easier to consistently take good care of someone you really love.

By all means, commit to evolving into the best, most

authentic, greatest version of yourself over the course of this lifetime. But love yourself now, exactly as you are. Celebrate your strengths, connect to the learning from all your experience, and bring your whole self to your authentic adventure. You deserve nothing less.

Lead with love

As our explorations come to an end, you find yourself on the brink of a new beginning. If you take these ideas to heart and commit to living your own authentic adventure, untold discoveries of your own await you. By seeing yourself with new eyes, you will see fresh possibilities in the world around you – the potential to lead yourself forward on your own terms and to live life fully, freely and with joy.

This book is, at its heart, about authentic self-leadership, which is the best possible preparation for leading others. Leadership allows you to grow the scope and impact of your contribution from one-to-few to one-to-many. And by being willing to share your journey, acknowledging setbacks as well as successes and allowing yourself to be truly seen, you will inspire courage and authenticity in those around you.

Share this book with a friend or colleague. Pull a 'power question' from its pages and explore it as a team. By training your own attention towards your own strengths and untapped potential, you will naturally see more clearly the brilliance in those around you. And by reflecting their unique and authentic gifts back to them – *their* zone of genius – you potentially inspire the next generation in the direction of their own authentic adventures.

And in those moments where you still don't know what to *do*, find certainty in knowing how you want to *be*. Lead with love, empathy and appreciation – inspiring hope, possibility and connectedness wherever you go – and the rest will follow.

Your ultimate destination

The ideas, strategies and stories I've shared in this book are my heartfelt attempt to support you in embracing the preciousness of every moment: claiming this journey as your own, and bringing it to life with your own gifts, your own passions and your own desire to make a difference.

I set out with the intention of helping you to transcend the destructive and debilitating paradigm that frames life – particularly corporate life – as a win–lose race, by offering you the more inspiring and empowering perspective of life as an authentic win–learn adventure. And most of all, I hoped to help you begin to see your own magnificence, and to inspire curiosity and a willingness to explore and express your unique gifts and talents every day, for your own joy and to the benefit of the world.

It is easy to overestimate what can be achieved in a day, a week or even a month. But it is equally easy to underestimate what can be *joyfully* achieved over the course of a year, a decade or a lifetime fully lived.

Over time, as your journey unfolds, each dream destination you reach will also be the starting point for a whole new authentic adventure. Each ending is also a new beginning, and that's not just the stuff of sequels and prequels. I know from my own and my clients' experience you'll be transformed by every authentic adventure you complete and inspired to make an even greater difference as a result, driving an *upward spiral of growth and contribution.*

The authentic and inspiring alternative to the old rules of the road this book provides is not only a route map for the dream destination that is calling you forwards *now*, but also your route map to *greatness*, however you would wish to define that.

Your greatest *life*, lived by the greatest version of you.

It is my sincere hope that something in these pages has inspired you to embrace the preciousness of your journey of a lifetime. Magic happens when you bring the same level of commitment to loving here as you were trained to bring to getting there.

BIBLIOGRAPHY

Achor, S. (2010). *The Happiness Advantage: The Seven Principles That Fuel Success and Performance at Work.* Virgin Books.

Allcott, G. (2015). *How to be a Productivity Ninja: Worry Less, Achieve More and Love What You Do.* Icon Books.

Brown, B. (2015). *Daring Greatly: How the Courage to be Vulnerable Transforms the Way We Live, Love, Parent and Lead.* Penguin Life.

Coelho, P. (1995). *The Alchemist.* HarperCollins.

Doyle, G. (2020). *Untamed: Stop Pleasing, Start Living.* Vermilion.

Duckworth. A. (2017). *Grit: Why passion and resilience are the secrets to success.* Vermilion.

Dweck, C.S. (2012). *Mindset: Changing the way you think to fulfil your potential.* Robinson.

Edwards, G. (2009). *Pure Bliss: The art of living in soft time.* Piatkus.

Edwards, G. (2009). *Wild Love: Discover the magical secrets of freedom, joy and unconditional love.* Piatkus.

Fields, J. (2021). *Sparked: Discover Your Unique Imprint for Work That Makes You Come Alive.* HarperCollins Leadership.

Garcia, H. & Miralles, F. (2017). *Ikigai: The Japanese secret to a long and happy life.* Hutchinson.

Finlay, G. (2007). *The Secret of Letting Go.* Llewellyn Publications.

Gilkey, C. (2019). *Start Finishing: How to Go from Idea to Done*. Sounds True Inc.

Gladwell, M. (2005). *Blink: The Power of Thinking Without Thinking*. Little, Brown & Company.

Hanson, R. (2009). *Buddha's Brain: The Practical Neuroscience of Happiness, Love and Wisdom*. New Harbinger.

Harari, Y.N. (2014). *Sapiens: A Brief History of Humankind*. Harvill Secker.

Hay, L. (2004). *Heal Your Body A-Z: The Mental Causes for Physical Illness and the Way to Overcome Them*. Hay House.

Hicks, E. & J. (2008). *The Astonishing Power of Emotions: Let Your Feelings Be Your Guide*. Hay House.

Katie, B. (2021). *Loving What Is: Four Questions That Can Change Your Life, Revised Edition*. Harmony.

Kahneman, D. (2012). *Thinking, Fast and Slow*. Penguin.

Knight, S. (2020). *NLP at Work: The Difference that Makes the Difference*. Fourth edition. Nicholas Brealey Publishing.

Maslow, A. (1966). *The Psychology of Science*. Harper & Row.

Mohr, T. (2015). *Playing Big: A practical guide for brilliant women like you*. Penguin.

Neff, K. (2011). *Self Compassion: The Proven Power of Being Kind to Yourself*. Yellow Kite.

Nestor, J. (2021). *Breath: The New Science of a Lost Art*. Penguin Life.

O'Mara, S. (2020). *In Praise of Walking: the new science of how we walk and why it's good for us*. Vintage.

Pressfield, S. (2003). *The War of Art: Break through the blocks, and win your inner creative battles*. Orion.

Ricard, M. (2012). *Happiness: A Guide to Developing Life's Most Important Skill*. Atlantic Books.

Robbins, M. (2017). *The 5 Second Rule: Transform Your Life, Work, and Confidence with Everyday Courage.* Savio Republic.

Saujani, R. (2019). *Brave, Not Perfect: Fear Less, Fail More, Live Bolder.* HQ.

Seligman, M.E.P. (2011). *Flourish: A New Understanding of Happiness and Well-being, and How to Achieve Them.* Nicholas Brealey Publishing.

Tieger, P. & Barron-Tieger, B. (2021). *Do What You Are: Discover the Perfect Career for You Through the Secrets of Personality Type.* Revised edition. Little, Brown & Company.

Wax, R. (2018). *How to Be Human: The Manual.* Penguin.

Williams, N. (2012). *Resisting Your Soul: A Handbook for Inspired Entrepreneurs.* Balloon View.

Wise, A. (2000). *The High Performance Mind: Mastering Brainwaves for Insight, Healing, and Creativity.* Jeremy P. Tarcher.

Recommended resources

Profiling tools

MBTIonline.com Online portal for Myers-Briggs personality profiling. Highly recommend working with a qualified practitioner where possible, and completing a guided self-assessment to find your best-fit personality type.

16Personalities.com Character profiling tool, similar to Myers-Briggs, also based on Jungian psychology.

Sparketype.com Archetype-based assessment of authentic work preferences.

EverythingDisc.com Information and assessment using the Wiley DiSC profiling tool.

ViaCharacter.org Character strengths assessment tool, highlighting the qualities and personality facets that make you feel most authentic and engaged.

Gallup.com/CliftonStrengths/en/254033/strengthsfinder.aspx Clifton Strengths profiling tool that signposts towards current strengths and offers guidance to cultivate untapped talents into strengths.

StrengthsProfile.com Strengths profiling tool that differentiates between innate strengths that energise you and learned strengths that drain you.

Other resources

KateTrafford.com For further resources to support your journey with this book, and to find out more about Kate's work supporting emerging leaders and purpose-driven organisations.

YouTube.com/watch?v=UF8uR6Z6KLc Video and full transcript of Steve Jobs' 15-minute speech at the Stanford Commencement Ceremony in 2005.

YouTube.com/watch?v=Lp7E973zozc Video of Mel Robbins' 2011 TEDx talk featuring the '5 second rule'.

Toastmasters.org Toastmasters International is a non-profit educational organisation that teaches public speaking and leadership skills through a worldwide network of in person and online clubs. A safe space to stretch yourself to learn, connect and have fun.

MeetUp.com Find people who share your interests through online and local in-person events.

ACKNOWLEDGEMENTS

The ideas in this book have been percolating in my heart and mind for close to 15 years. And yet, it was only once I began writing that I discovered how true it is that writing a book is a team effort. My heartfelt thanks go to the following members of my incredible convoy:

My husband Tony and 'beloved offspring' Jess and Emily, who cheered me on, reminded me to get out of my own way and celebrated every magical milestone.

My teacher, coach and mentor, John Overdurf, for being the Yoda to my Skywalker for over two decades, helping me to find my way.

The publishing team at The Right Book Company: Paul, Andrew, Caroline and Beverley, who each played a part in shaping these ideas and in making this book a thing of beauty. Special thanks to Sue Richardson, who guided me forwards during the daunting first draft stage, and helped me find my authentic voice as a first-time writer. Thanks too to independent designer Hannah Nolloth for the wonderful illustrations.

My RBC 'Book Buddies' – Nadine, Nick, Richard, Ceri, Darren, David, William, Mike and Jan – who showed up for hour upon hour of early morning co-writing magic and tested, challenged and celebrated my insights along the way.

My beta readers – Cat, Alaine, Mark, Angela, Andy, Eleanor, Lynsey, Jo, Christina and Abbe – who took time out of their very busy lives to read my raw manuscript and told me what worked and what didn't.

To the many authors, teachers, clients and colleagues who have helped me grow and my ideas to evolve over the course of many years and inspired me to make this contribution of my own.

And finally to you, dear reader, for making it this far. Thank you for having the curiosity to explore what success means to you, the courage to dream big, and the authenticity to commit to getting there *and* loving here. In the beautiful words of the traditional Irish farewell blessing,

**'May the road rise up to meet you,
and the wind always be at your back'.**

About the Author

Kate Trafford is a Master Coach, author and TEDx speaker on the subject of authentic success. She has over 20 years' experience helping business leaders and their teams drive for big results – *and* love the journey.

Kate specialises in designing and delivering bespoke Talent Development programmes for organisations wanting to support and accelerate the growth of their emerging leaders. She is an enthusiastic advocate of sustainable success, working to ensure her clients set themselves up for both significant impact in the short run *and* authentic happiness for the long haul. You can find out more about Kate's work at **www.KateTrafford.com**

How did she get here? After qualifying as a chartered engineer and later working in government relations, Kate shifted her passion for personal development from the side-lines to the centre of her work. She created and led 'power skills' workshops on personal effectiveness, impact and influence, and creative problem-solving. Later, as a coach, she became fascinated by the ways we unconsciously limit our own success and happiness. She discovered many little-known secrets of how to release this resistance – so progress can be both swift and enjoyable – qualifying along the way as a Master Hypnotherapist.

Kate lives with her husband in Cheshire, England. She is a proud mum to two amazing young adults, and to two very fluffy Bichons.